AF328607

EILEEN MAYO

This book is from a series about Modern Women Artists
published by Eiderdown Books.

Other titles available from the same series:



To order books, please visit eiderdownbooks.com

# EILEEN MAYO

## Sara Cooper

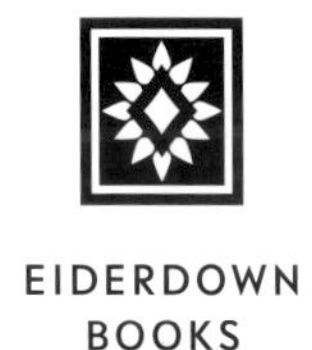

EIDERDOWN
BOOKS

MODERN WOMEN ARTISTS

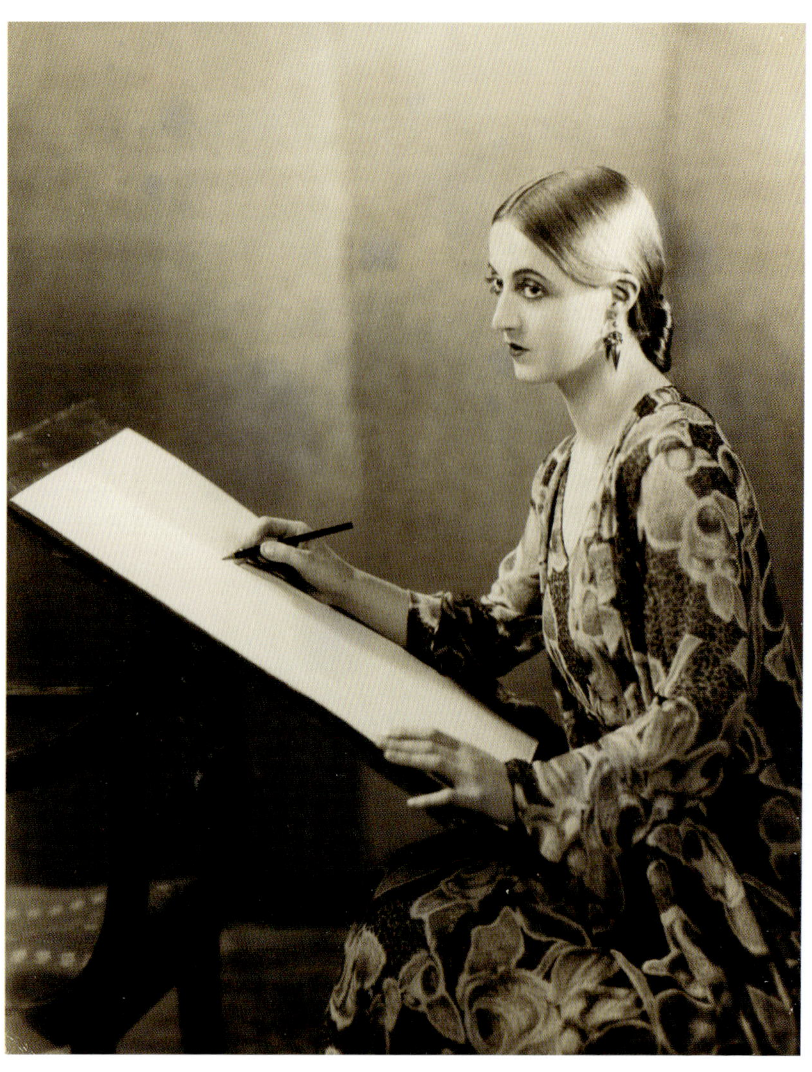

**1.** Studio portrait photograph of Eileen Mayo by Marion Hoppé, c.1920–40

Eileen Mayo (1906–94) was a talented and multi-skilled painter, printmaker, tapestry designer, and illustrator. She had a deep-held fascination with natural history that shines through her work across all media. She was also an adventurer – travelling widely and frequently from Britain to South Africa, Germany, Australia and New Zealand – pursuing her art, but also perhaps as an escape from the stability of a domestic life that she was expected to fulfil, like so many women of her generation.

Mayo was also an artist's model, and for a time became one of the most sought-after sitters of the early twentieth century, depicted in paintings by some of the leading lights in modern British art, including Dod and Ernest Procter, Bernard Meninsky, and as the 'Golden Girl' for Laura and Harold Knight.

As an artist, Mayo is better known today in Australia and New Zealand – the two countries to which she emigrated in 1952 and 1962 respectively, and where her work has been celebrated in exhibitions and acquired by public collections. In Britain, she was made a Dame in 1994 for services to the arts, awarded just three days before she died. This was a late recognition of her wide contribution to art and design, but since then, in this country at least, Mayo's work has all but faded from public view.

## Early Life

Born in Norwich on 11 September 1906 to Hubert and Violet Mayo, Eileen was followed by her sisters Margery in 1909 and Josephine in 1913. Hubert's teaching posts lead the family to relocate to Wakefield and then to Bristol in 1918. When her family moved again to Cheshire two years later, Eileen remained in Bristol, boarding at Clifton High School. In 1921, Hubert died aged 41 having contracted meningitis, and a few years after his death, Mayo's mother and sisters emigrated to New Zealand, while she remained in Britain. Frequent relocation during her childhood, the death of her father, and her mother's subsequent emigration may well have contributed to the independence, self-sufficiency and single-minded pursuit of her art that drove Mayo for the rest of her life.

Mayo was an introverted and shy child, who possessed an 'anxious perfectionism and predilection for making every task as difficult as possible to prove both her personal integrity as well as her artistic worth both to herself and to those around her,' but she demonstrated an early appreciation of nature.[1]

From January to October 1920, Mayo kept a daily nature diary, recording observations of weather conditions, emerging flora and fauna and sightings of birds and animals.[2] Pages of skilled botanic illustrations accompany her hand-written notes: 'Found the following flowers:- Celandine, Periwinkle, dead nettle, gorse, violets, daisies & Laurestina. Daffodils were out in one garden'.[3]

Her ability to recognise plant species, identify bird calls, insect types and reference weather patterns demonstrated an understanding of the natural world that belied her young age. The reassuring inevitability of the changing seasons must have served as an anchor and solace to a young Mayo, in contrast to the background of her unsettled home life. Her early botanic drawings would also provide a rich resource for her later artworks.

Academically, Mayo was an exceptional student. A family friend and headmaster of the nearby Bristol Grammar School, Mr J.E. Barton, along with Eileen's art teacher Miss Rentoul, recognised her outstanding creative talents and encouraged her to apply to the Slade.[4] With its progressive approach, encouragement of women and strong focus on drawing, it was felt Mayo would flourish in this art college, and would receive the most rigorous artistic training. Mayo enrolled in 1923 under Henry Tonks and alongside future artists such as Mary Adshead, Winifred Knights, Hilda Carline and Eileen Agar.

However, disillusionment with the Slade quickly emerged, as limited financial means and her naturally introverted nature set her apart from fellow students. She also found the teaching lacking and criticism far from constructive, especially from Tonks. Furthermore, Mayo's access to the life-drawing rooms was limited, not because of restrictions around the entry of women, but conversely because the sheer number of women enrolled at this time meant that the women's life-room was full, and it was difficult to get close to the model. Increasingly she spent her time at the Victoria and Albert Museum (V&A), the British Museum, Kew Gardens or the London Zoo, teaching herself through drawing and refocusing on her love of the natural world.

Leaving the Slade in 1925 to concentrate on more applied applications of her artistic skills, Mayo enrolled in evening classes at the Central School of Arts and Crafts. Here she found the combination of teaching design and craft, as well as fine art, and a focus on practical skill-building in areas such as calligraphy, wood-engraving and printmaking, to be far more aligned with her own interests, and she remained at the college until 1928. With limited financial income, she took on a variety of minor commissions for adverts, book jackets and posters.[5]

Even though Mayo had been living independently in London since starting at the Slade, when her mother and sisters emigrated to New Zealand in 1926 it must have given Eileen, aged only 20, the awareness that forging a career as a professional artist – and artist's model – would be key to providing her with much-needed financial stability.

# Life as an Artist's Model

Her time as model to some of the key artists of the 1920s is critical in appreciating the path of Mayo's own artistic career. She started by posing for life classes while at college, but gradually became sought-after by more established artists and began working privately from their studios.

A magazine image of a painting by Dame Laura Knight, in which the sitter shared a remarkable likeness to herself, prompted Mayo to contact Knight offering to model for her. It was the start of a warm friendship and working relationship between the two women that lasted for many years, as reflected in their numerous letters discussing their art but also exchanging gifts, recipes and dressmaking patterns.

Mayo accompanied Laura and her husband, the painter Harold Knight, to Cornwall every summer for the next four years. They called her the 'Golden Girl' and she was the subject of some of their finest portraits (Fig. 2).[6] During this period she was also painted by Dod and Ernest Procter, Bernard Meninsky and Edith Lawrence, and posed for Duncan Grant and Vanessa Bell at their Fitzroy Street studio. Mayo seemed particularly drawn to, and comfortable around, women artists, particularly Laura Knight and Dod Procter, who were older than her and treated her with great kindness. Notably it is only in paintings for these artists that she is painted nude.

Pragmatic about her role as a model, Mayo used each of her jobs as an opportunity to learn from these accomplished artists: 'All the time I have been posing for painters I have been studying their methods and listening to their talk. In this way I have learned far more than I have ever learned in an art school'.[7] This network of artists was well-connected, sociable and willing to help and support a younger generation, and would have been encouraging of Mayo's artistic work and career. It was through Laura Knight that Mayo would receive her first major commission.

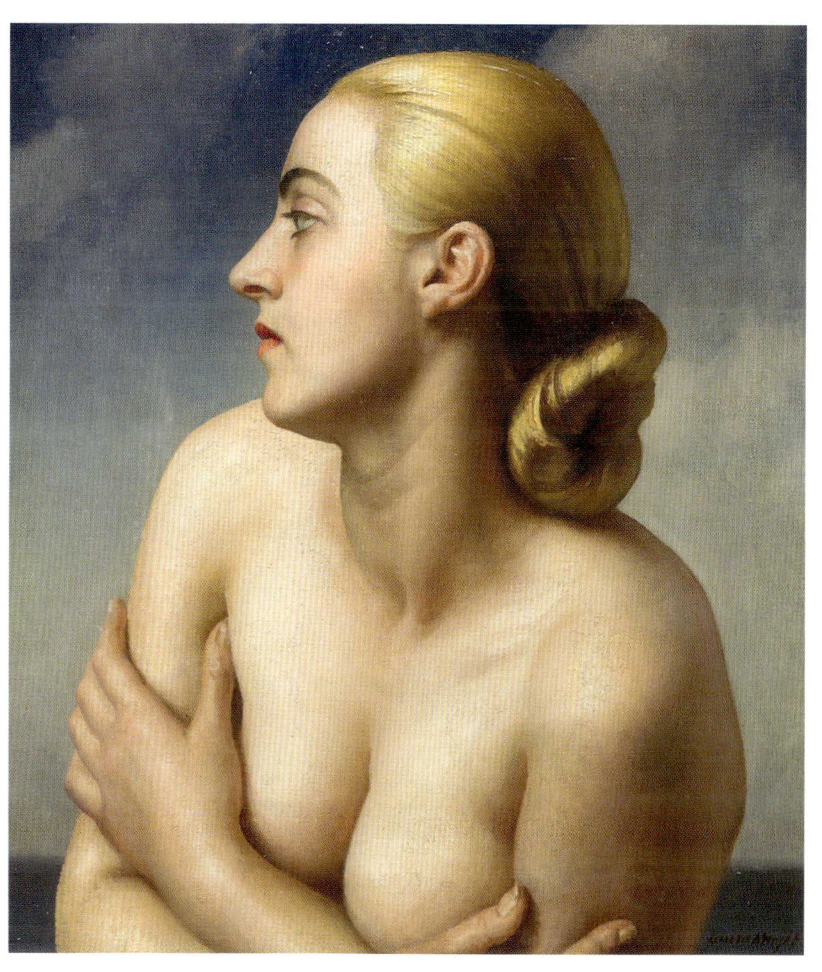

2. Laura Knight, *Blue and Gold*, 1927, oil on canvas

## Early Commissions

In 1927 Knight introduced Mayo to Cyril Beaumont, founder of the Beaumont Press. During the 1920s there was a peak of interest in ballet, and Beaumont had written and published a number of books on the subject, in particular regarding the Ballets Russes, where Knight had worked backstage sketching the dancers.[8] In a series of booklets about the Diaghilev ballet, Beaumont included a number of hand-coloured prints, initially colouring them with his wife Alice, but later inviting artists including Mayo, Randolf Schwabe and Ethelbert White to assist in this process.[9] Mayo appreciated Beaumont's ambition for the illustrations to be simple and accurate representations of the ballet scenes, executed as precise line drawings (Fig. 3).

However, it was the simplicity in this work, and in a number of her other early prints, that began to reveal Mayo's lack of training in figure-drawing. Determined to overcome her perceived shortcomings, she signed up for life-drawing classes, first at the Westminster School of Art under Bernard Meninsky, and later with Henry Moore at Chelsea Polytechnic.

Her first major solo commission – a book cover for the Beaumont Press,[10] was a great success and reviewed as being 'the most effective piece of design and colour in the book'.[11] For *A Japanese Garland*, a collection of poems, Mayo produced delicate yet stylised designs with the emphasis on black line and the soft colouring typical of historic Japanese prints.[12] The 1930 children's Christmas publication *Toys* included Mayo's charming, brightly coloured illustrations representing a toy for each letter of the alphabet.[13] Again these were well-received and highly praised in the press, and from this point on, Mayo's reputation as an illustrator was established.[14]

3. Serge Lifar in George Balanchine's ballet *Apollo Musagetes*, Diaghilev Ballets Russes, 1928, drawing on paper

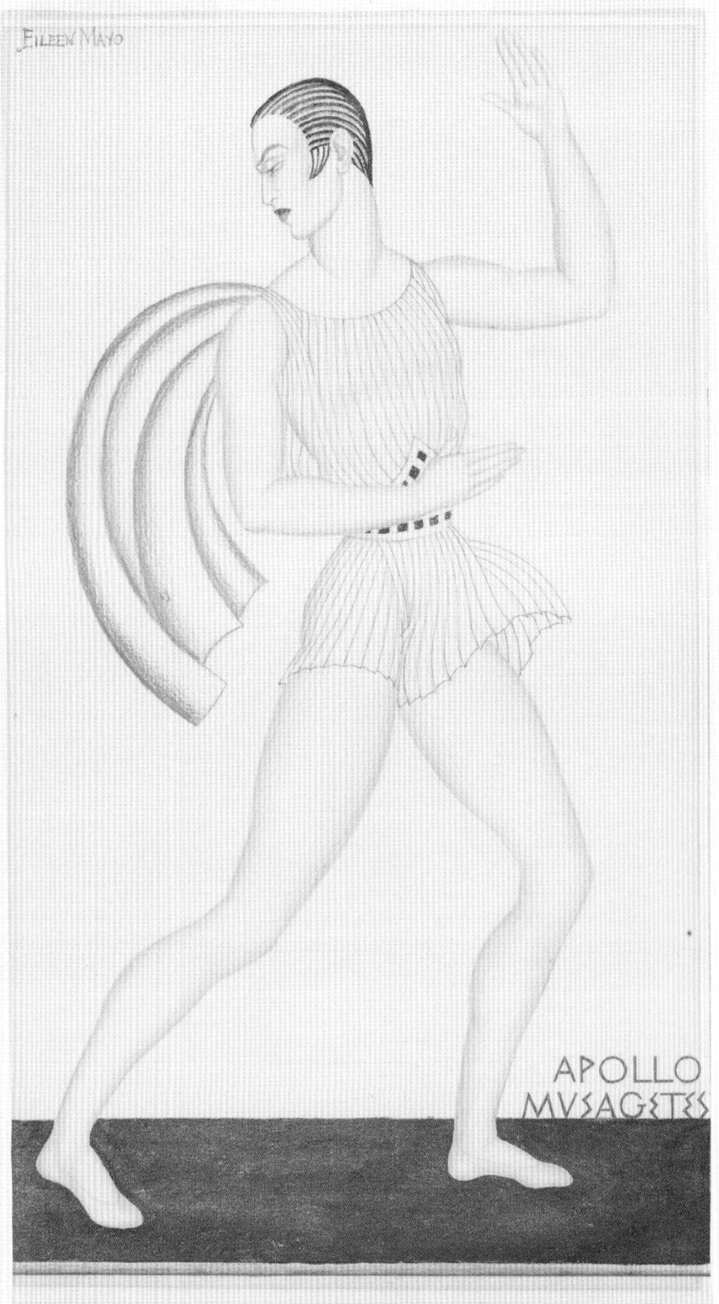

EILEEN MAYO
APOLLO
MVSAGETES

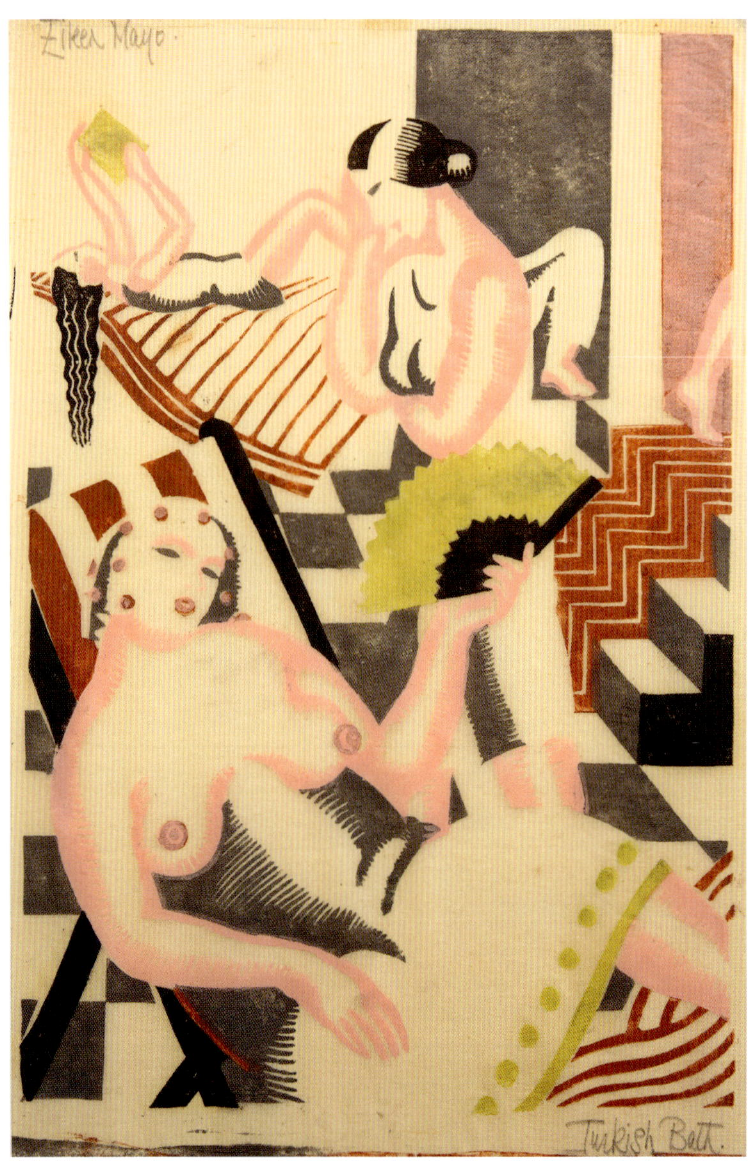


4. *Turkish Bath*, 1930, 4-colour lino-cut

Mayo joined the life-class at the Grosvenor School of Modern Art in 1929. This new art school was jointly run by the wood-engraver Iain Macnab, and Claude Flight, who taught colour lino-cutting. Students included Sybil Andrews and Cyril Power, and the school became central to a revival of interest in printmaking in Britain between the wars.

Her friendship with Flight was perhaps the closest Mayo came to an association with an artists' group. The two lived close to each other in north London and would often discuss their respective commissions; Flight was encouraging and constructive in his advice to Mayo.[15] Having previous experience of wood-engraving, the transfer of skills to lino-cutting would not have been a challenge for Mayo, as the techniques were similar. However, what she leant from Flight was how to over-print in several colours – a technique that he once explained to her over the telephone.

At Flight's invitation, Mayo exhibited in the *Second Exhibition of British Lino-Cuts* at the Redfern Gallery in 1930, which proved an important turning point for her.[16] Still at an early stage in her career, Mayo was inexperienced and reluctant to draw attention to herself and risk criticism. In this show, among 43 other artists, she was able to show her work without the pressure of expectation. The result was the 4-colour block lino-cut *Turkish Bath* (Fig. 4) – a delightful depiction of women enjoying the sociable bathing experience popular at this time. Mayo worked with her usual perfectionism on the piece, recounting in an interview that 'I had to work 18 hours a day . . . I was lucky to have it included. I was almost too late. I wasn't pleased with one of the blocks and I cut it four times. The delay nearly proved fatal to my success.'[17]

Encouraged by the exhibition, Mayo made several more prints, including *Woman at a Dressing Table* (1931, Fig. 5), *Morning Tea* (1932), *Ice Cream Cart* (1932), *The Two Angelos* (1934), and *Doric Dairy* (1935, Fig. 6), most of which were again shown at the Redfern Gallery. Acknowledging her ambition to become a full-time artist she explained:

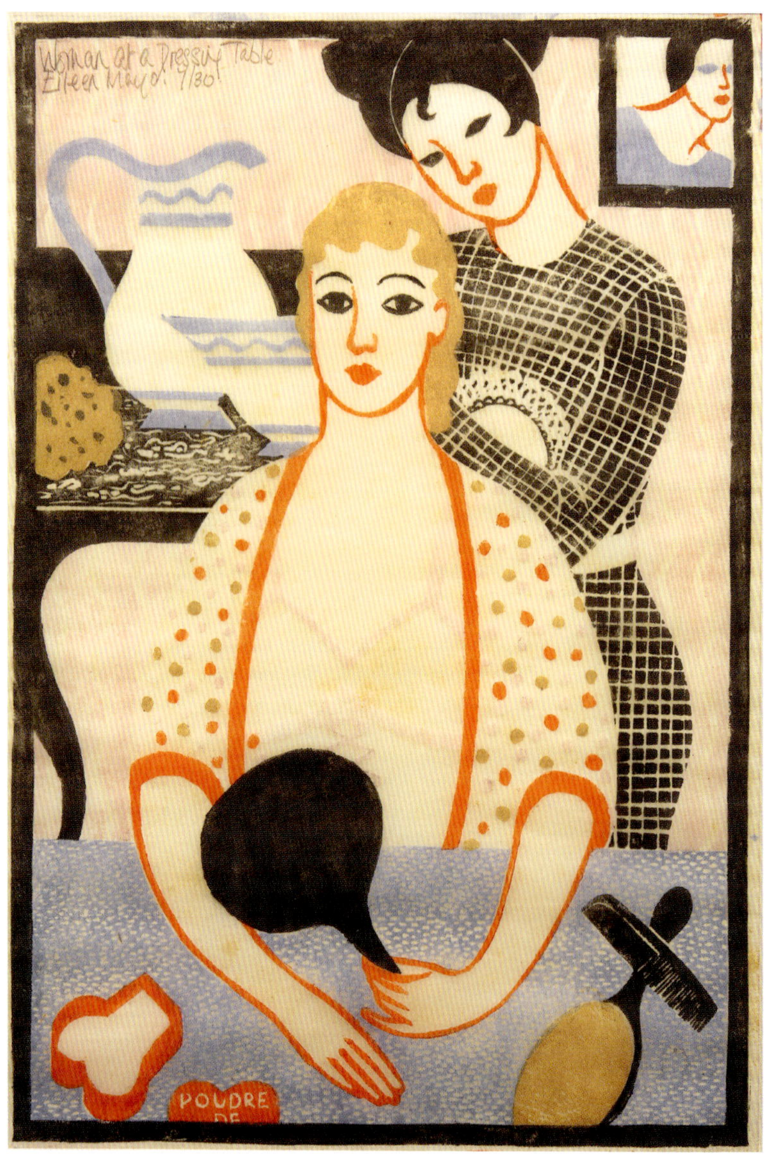


**5.** *Woman at a Dressing Table*, 1931, 5-colour lino-cut

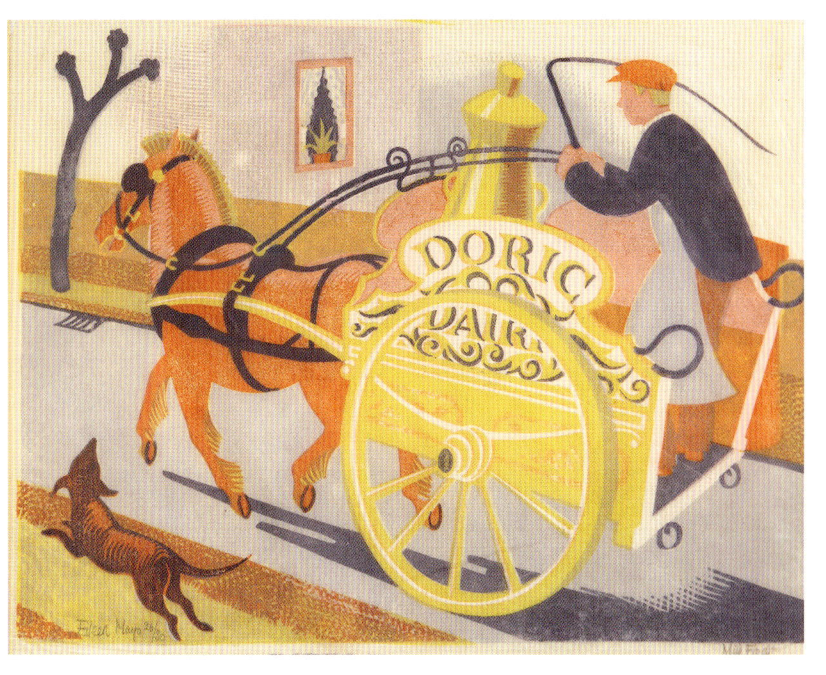

**6.** *Doric Dairy*, 1935, 5-colour lino-cut

I have almost entirely given up posing as a model. I want to be a painter, and now that people are beginning to buy my work I have great hopes. I don't think I shall ever have the heart to have a model myself. I know only too well the difficulties and the strain of posing. Besides, after a long day on the studio I often come home and get on with my own painting far into the night.[18]

The association with Flight and the avant-garde lino-cut group, regular exhibitions at the Redfern Gallery, her developing self-confidence and a more comfortable financial situation meant that for this short period in the late 1920s, Mayo's work felt more modern, spontaneous and experimental than at any other point in her career.

## Travel and Adventure

Just as Mayo was establishing herself as a notable artist and printmaker, the 1930s bought a change in fortune. The 1929 Wall Street crash and subsequent economic slump led to a shrinking of the freelance illustration opportunities that had provided her with a basic income. Rather than following purely commercial commissions, Mayo decided instead to travel, and in 1931 took a job looking after the children of a Greek family in Wiesbaden, Germany, using the opportunity to visit the public museums and galleries there and in Berlin. The pay from her post must have been significant as she bought herself a square negative format Voigtländer camera of which, according to her stepson, she was very proud.[19] From this point on, several of her photos (now held in the Tate archive and with the family) were square format and likely to have been taken with this camera, including those from her subsequent journey to Africa.

At this time, visiting Europe, while adventurous, was not unusual, but her next trip showed a certain bravery and disregard for convention that was quietly upheld by Mayo

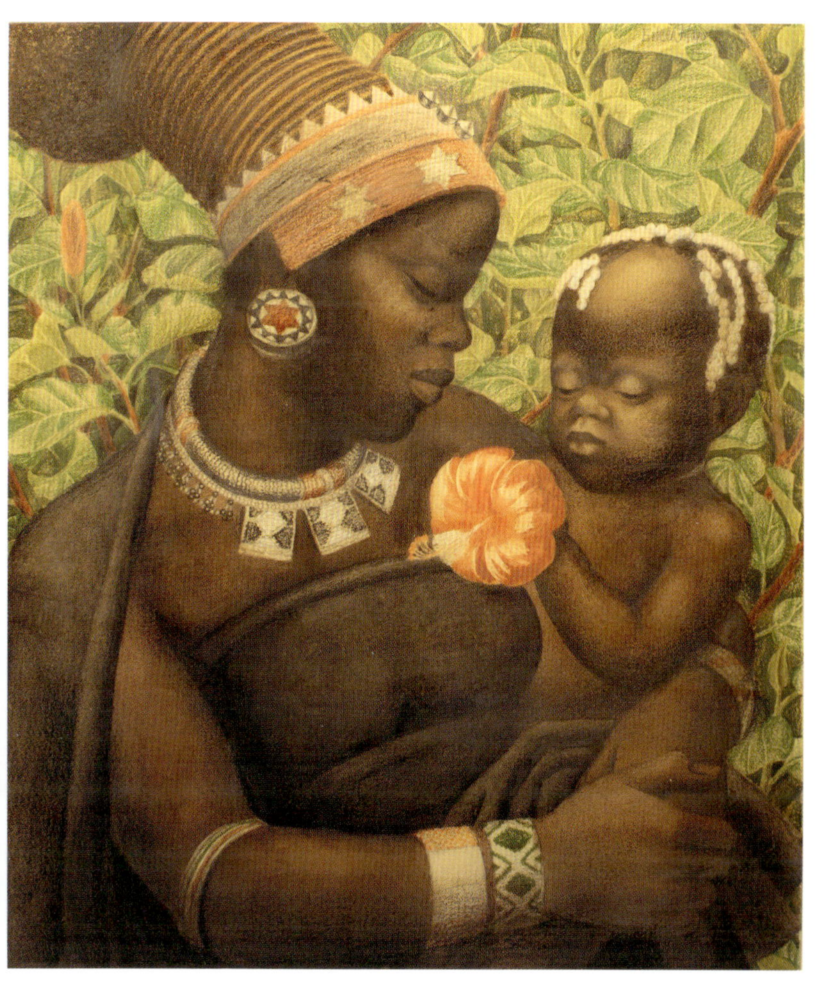

**7.** *Zulu Mother and Child*, 1935, conte crayon on card

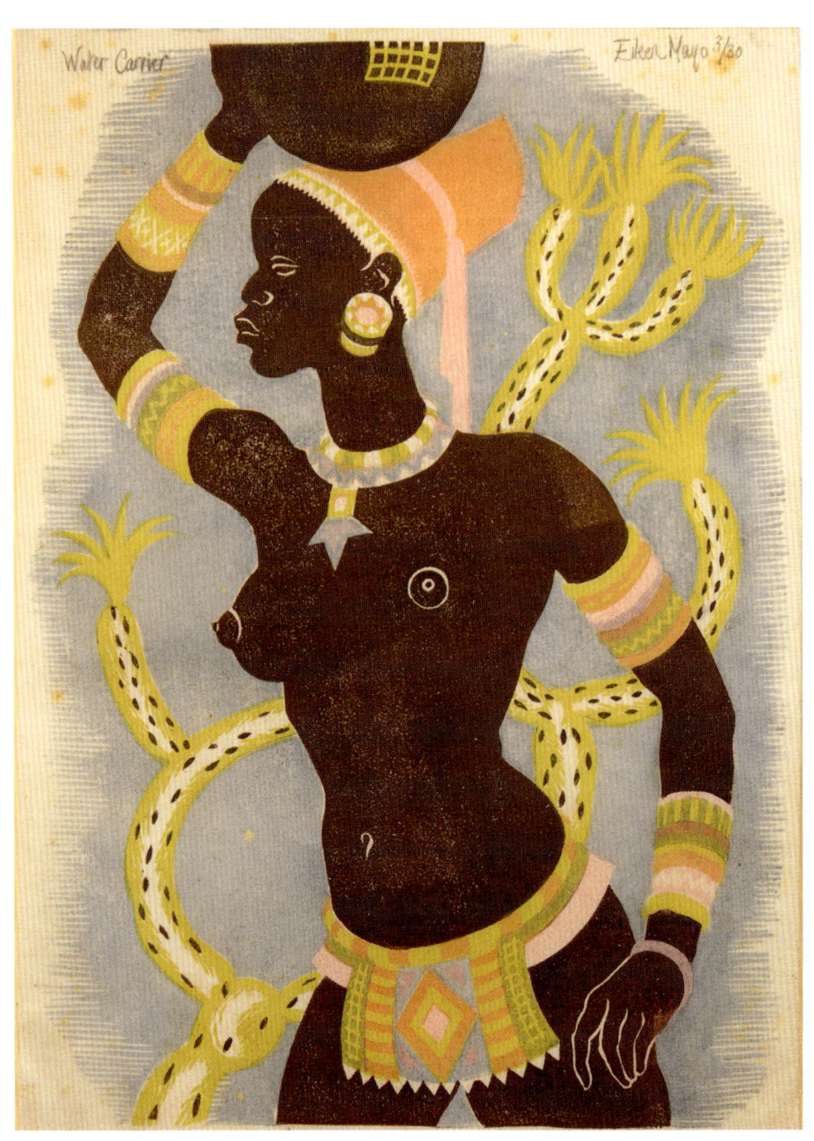



8. *Water Carrier*, 1937, 4-colour lino-cut

throughout her life. Responding to an invitation to visit her cousin in Durban, she booked onto the *Usaramo*, a German East Africa Line passenger and cargo ship. It departed from Southampton on the 11 October 1934 and sailed around Africa, docking at several ports en route. During the trip Mayo spent time in Cape Town, taking the opportunity to see some of the unique flora and fauna of South Africa, which she found fascinating. In her large sketchpad she made numerous drawings of Zulu women, including careful observations and notes that she would later use in her studio.

Mayo's African sketchbooks would provide an inspiring resource, and on her return to Britain in 1935, she produced a collection of paintings and prints, including several botanic illustrations and depictions of the women she had met on her trip. Delicately drawn works such as *Zulu Mother and Child* (1935, Fig. 7), and the coloured lithograph *Water Carrier* (1937, Fig. 8) show Mayo celebrating the beauty of motherhood and revering the strength of the women going about their work.

## Settled in Sussex

The mid-1930s brought more change. In 1936 Mayo met and married Dr Richard Gainsborough and moved into his home in St John's Wood, London. Ralph, as he was known, had a young son, John, from a previous marriage and Eileen not only embraced married life but also that of becoming a stepmother. Marriage and financial security after years of uncertainty must have appealed to her, enabling artistic pathways not previously explored for fear of the financial risks attached to failure.[20]

One commission came from the BBC radio producer and publisher Douglas Cleverdon,[21] who invited Mayo to illustrate the 1937 publication *The Bamboo Dancer and Other African Tales*,[22] a series of previously unpublished folk stories for which she produced a set of eight coloured engravings. Drawing on

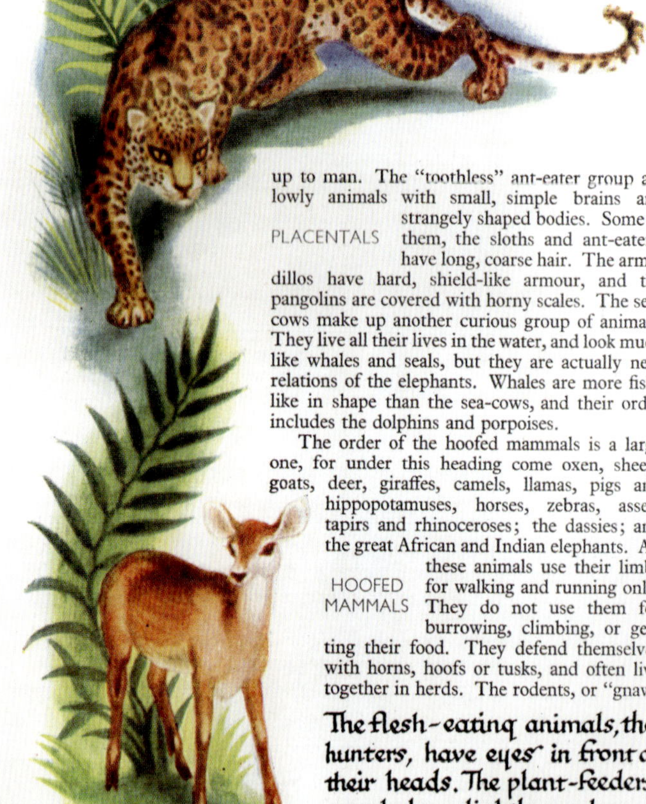

up to man. The "toothless" ant-eater group are lowly animals with small, simple brains and strangely shaped bodies. Some of PLACENTALS them, the sloths and ant-eaters, have long, coarse hair. The armadillos have hard, shield-like armour, and the pangolins are covered with horny scales. The seacows make up another curious group of animals. They live all their lives in the water, and look much like whales and seals, but they are actually near relations of the elephants. Whales are more fishlike in shape than the sea-cows, and their order includes the dolphins and porpoises.

The order of the hoofed mammals is a large one, for under this heading come oxen, sheep, goats, deer, giraffes, camels, llamas, pigs and hippopotamuses, horses, zebras, asses, tapirs and rhinoceroses; the dassies; and the great African and Indian elephants. All these animals use their limbs HOOFED for walking and running only. MAMMALS They do not use them for burrowing, climbing, or getting their food. They defend themselves with horns, hoofs or tusks, and often live together in herds. The rodents, or "gnaw-

**The flesh-eating animals, the hunters, have eyes in front of their heads. The plant-feeders' eyes bulge slightly and are at the sides of the head.**

166

9. *The Story of Living Things and their Evolution*
(Waverley Book Company, London 1944)

her first-hand knowledge of African flora and fauna as well as her figure studies of Zulu women, Mayo's designs for this project reveal a greater confidence in her own abilities than for any previous commissions.

By 1937 the family had moved to a farmhouse in Mannings Heath, near Horsham, West Sussex, with Mayo also maintaining the London home and travelling between the two. In Sussex, she took the opportunity to further her lithography skills, studying with the artist Vincent Lines at Horsham School of Art. However, as the 1930s progressed and fewer people bought prints, Mayo was mindful of the need to diversify her artistic practice and enrolled at Chelsea Polytechnic to study under Henry Moore and Robert Medley.[23] With war raging, the family moved again to Stroods – a country house in Fletching, East Sussex – where Gainsborough managed three GP practices with assistance from Mayo.

Increasingly during this wartime period, Mayo's domestic life demanded more of her time and her artistic practice was largely put aside. Painting materials were also harder to come by and so with her usual creativity and resilience, Mayo turned to writing and once again to illustration. Reviving her early passion for the natural world, she researched and wrote 300 pages of text and produced over 1,000 original illustrations for *The Story of Living Things and their Evolution* (Fig. 9).[24] In the foreword, Professor Julian Huxley wrote how 'Mayo's charming and unusual illustrations ... have the merit of being based on careful study of the facts of nature and of biological authorities, and with her equally careful text, combine to give an excellent presentation of evolutionary biology.' He goes on: 'the book can be commended as providing the layman with a picture of life's unfolding and of the rich variety it has produced, more vivid than most professional biologists could achieve.'[25] Against a background of war, life in the country had reignited a passion for nature that had been somewhat forsaken during Mayo's time in London.

The same year Mayo wrote and illustrated *Shells and how they live* (Fig. 10),[26] and in 1945, produced *Little Animals of the Countryside*[27] and *Larger Animals of the Countryside*,[28] all for Pleiades Books. Following the success of these publications, Pleiades commissioned illustrations for *One Day on Beetle Rock* by American naturalist and writer Sally Carrighar – a compilation of stories about nine animals that lived in Sequoia National Park.[29]

1945 also saw Mayo's first entries accepted into the Royal Academy Summer Exhibition.[30] She showed four works: two wood-engravings, a lino-cut, and a lithograph titled *Squirrel* (1945, Fig. 11). This hand-printed black and white lithograph clearly demonstrates the skill she brought to the technique, not only in the composition – which employed a dynamic diagonal from the squirrel's head in the lower right corner, curling up to the tail which frames the top left of the work – but also in the shadow and highlights used across the squirrel's back and tail, which suggested a softness to the fur. Mayo went on to produce further lithographs including *Musk Duck* (1945), which was included in the 1948 RA summer exhibition.[31]

These lithographic prints demonstrated a raising of Mayo's ambition in terms of scale and colour, as well as a shift in subject matter toward landscapes, aligning with her tempera painting of the same period. *Mending the Net* (1949, Fig. 12) and *Roquebrune* (1952), both larger-scale colour lithographs, were based on photographs Mayo had taken during trips to France. The first was taken on a family holiday to Audierne; the second during a four-month visit split between Paris and Roquebrune.[32] Her focus on lithography may have been facilitated by the purchase of a new house in Chelsea in 1947, the top floor of which was converted into an apartment and studio. Mayo installed a printing press in the studio, enabling her to concentrate on her work while in London.

**10.** *Shells and how they live* (Waverley Book Company, London 1944)

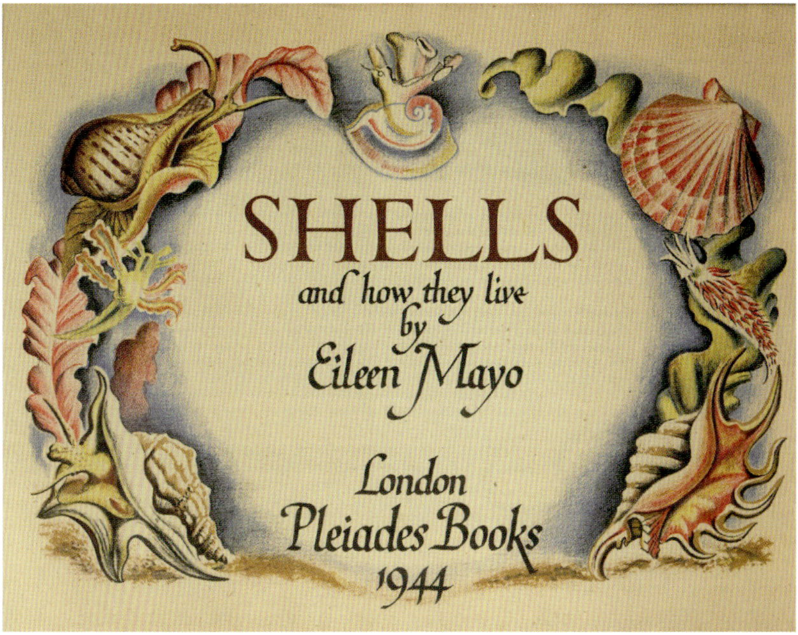

# SHELLS

and how they live
by
Eileen Mayo

London
Pleiades Books
1944

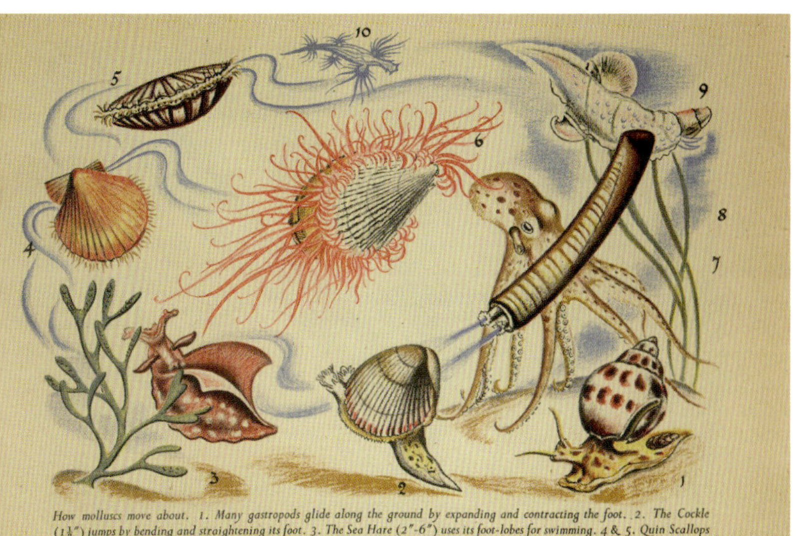

How molluscs move about. 1. Many gastropods glide along the ground by expanding and contracting the foot. 2. The Cockle (1½″) jumps by bending and straightening its foot. 3. The Sea Hare (2″-6″) uses its foot-lobes for swimming. 4 & 5. Quin Scallops (3″-5″) and 6. the File-shell (2″) swim by snapping the valves of their shells together. 7. The Razor-shell (8″) does the same and also shoots water out through its siphons. 8. Besides swimming the octopus walks on its arms. 9. Carinaria (4″-8″) moves its tail and finlike foot as it swims upside down. 10. Glaucus (1″) floats at the surface of the water.

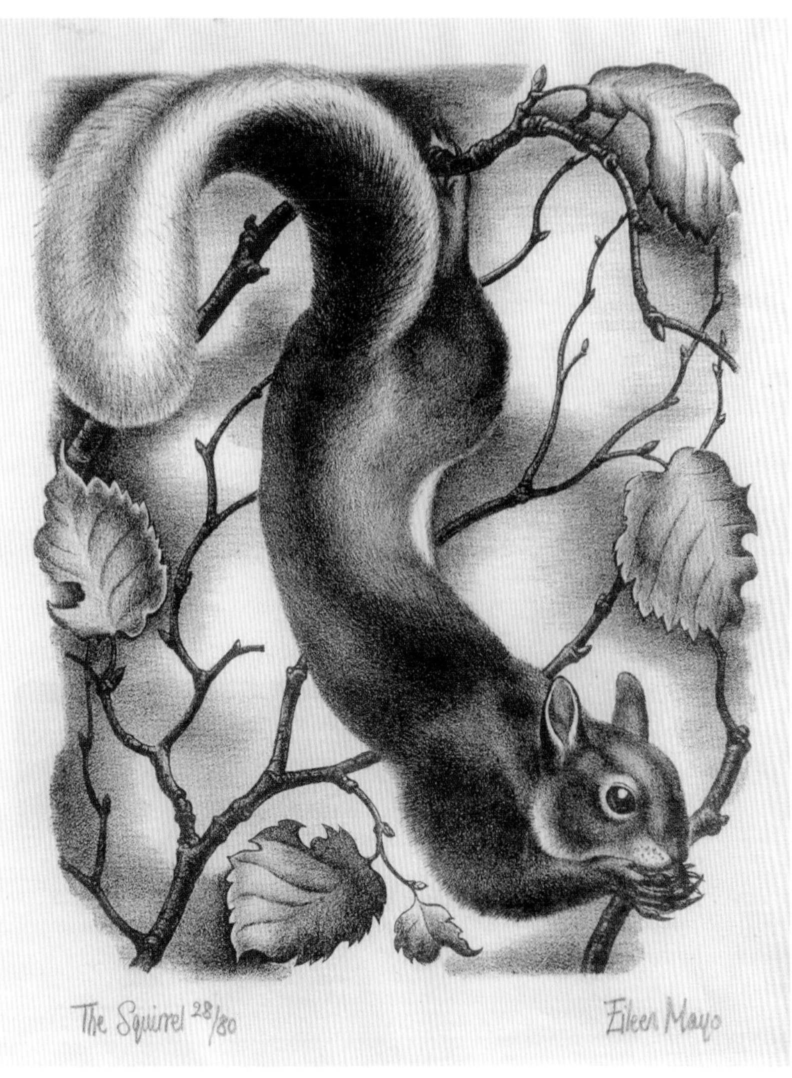



**11.** *Squirrel*, 1945, lithograph

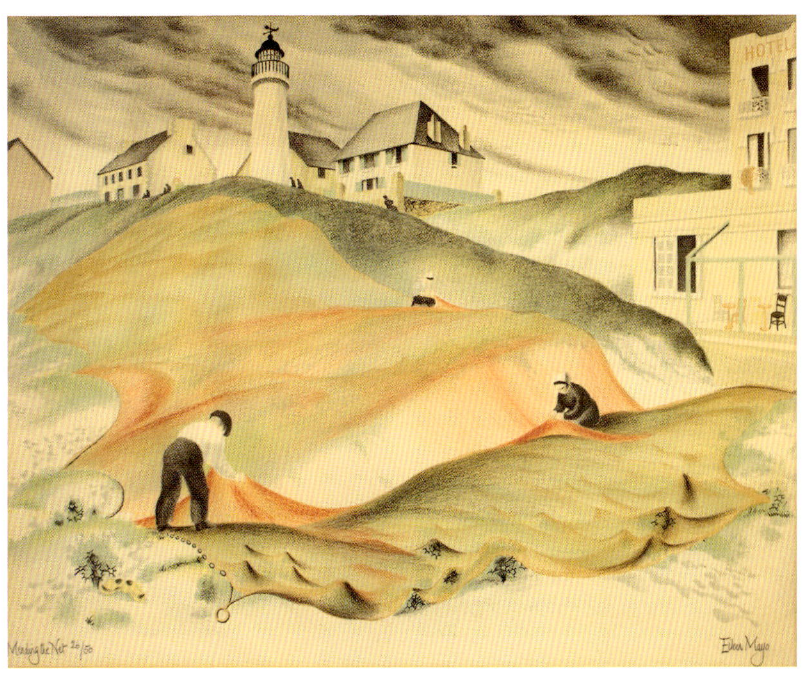



**12.** *Mending the Net*, 1949, lithograph

# Painting

At the outset of her career, Mayo was most interested in becoming a painter, perhaps a result of the time spent in Cornwall with Laura and Harold Knight (one of her earliest paintings is a small landscape titled *Mousehole* (1930), depicting the location close to their Cornish base).[33] On occasion she also spoke of her desire to be a painter: in 1940 she said, 'When I have finished enough panels, I am going to stage a one-man show in London, that will be my real come-back. I have exhibited paintings in London before but always with other artists.'[34]

Yet unlike printmaking and illustration, painting did not come naturally to Mayo, although she applied her inherent perfectionism in order to master it. As suggested by her biographer Dr Jillian Cassidy, this rigorousness may have been detrimental to her work on occasion, which sometimes lacked 'life'.[35] Mayo was not the most prolific painter and very few of her paintings are held in public collections. This perhaps goes some way to explain her relative anonymity as an artist in modern times, especially in the UK, rather than as an author and illustrator.

The oil paintings that Mayo produced during the 1940s, among them *Fletching Mill* (1941, Fig. 13), *Tabby Cat* (1948) and *Blue Nets* (1950, Fig. 14), overlap with the subject matter of her prints, taking landscape, seascapes and nature as their general themes. *Fletching Mill* is well-planned in its composition, with the mill building sitting central to the image, the road over the bridge leading towards the waterwheel reminiscent of some of the machinery depicted in the watercolours of Eric Ravilious. The heavy clouds and gentle landscape in the background are similar to those found in the post-First World War landscapes of John Nash.

Mayo was also fastidious in her use of egg tempera, which she preferred to oil paint, despite it being the more difficult

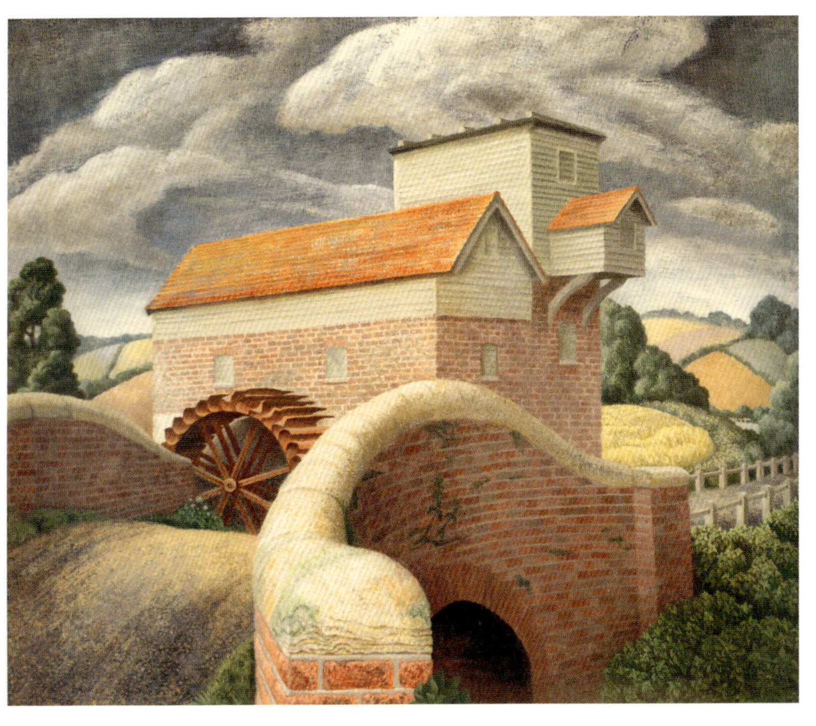

13. *Fletching Mill*, 1941, oil on canvas

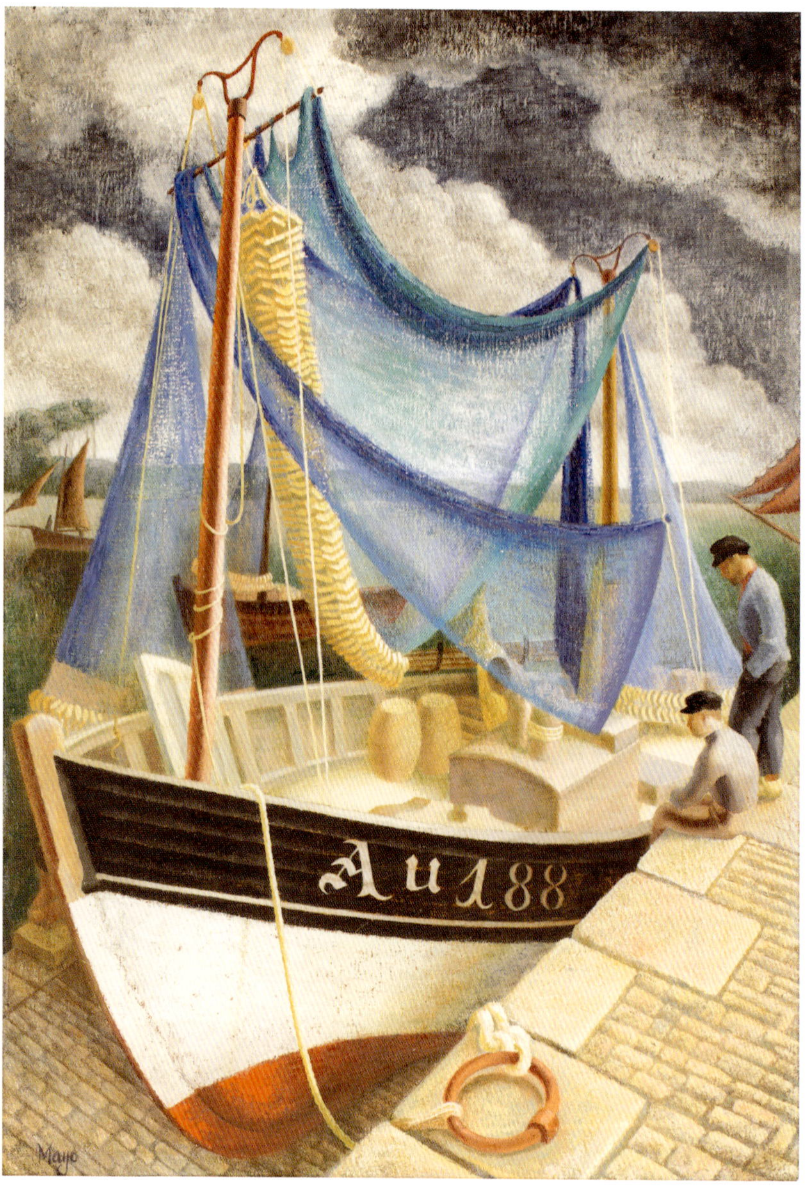

Mayo
Au188

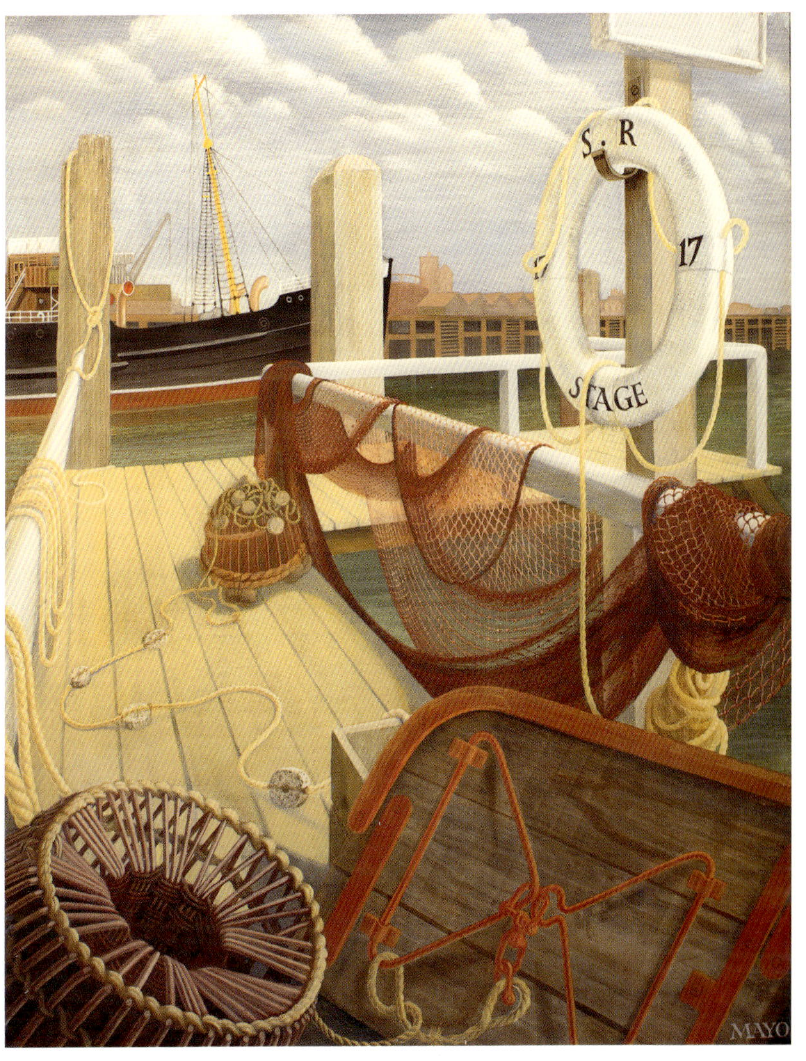


**14.** (opposite) *Blue Nets*, 1950, oil on canvas
**15.** (above) *Stage 17*, 1948, tempera on oak panel

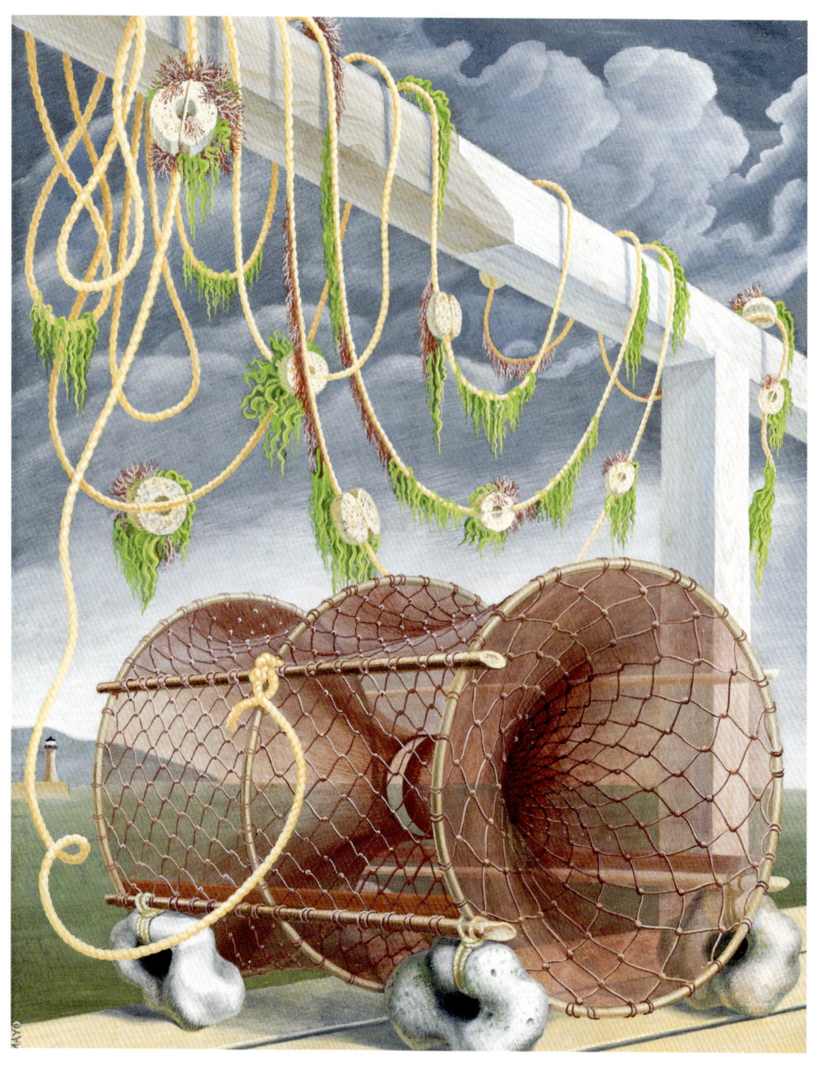

**16.** *Lobster Pot*, 1950, tempera on oak panel

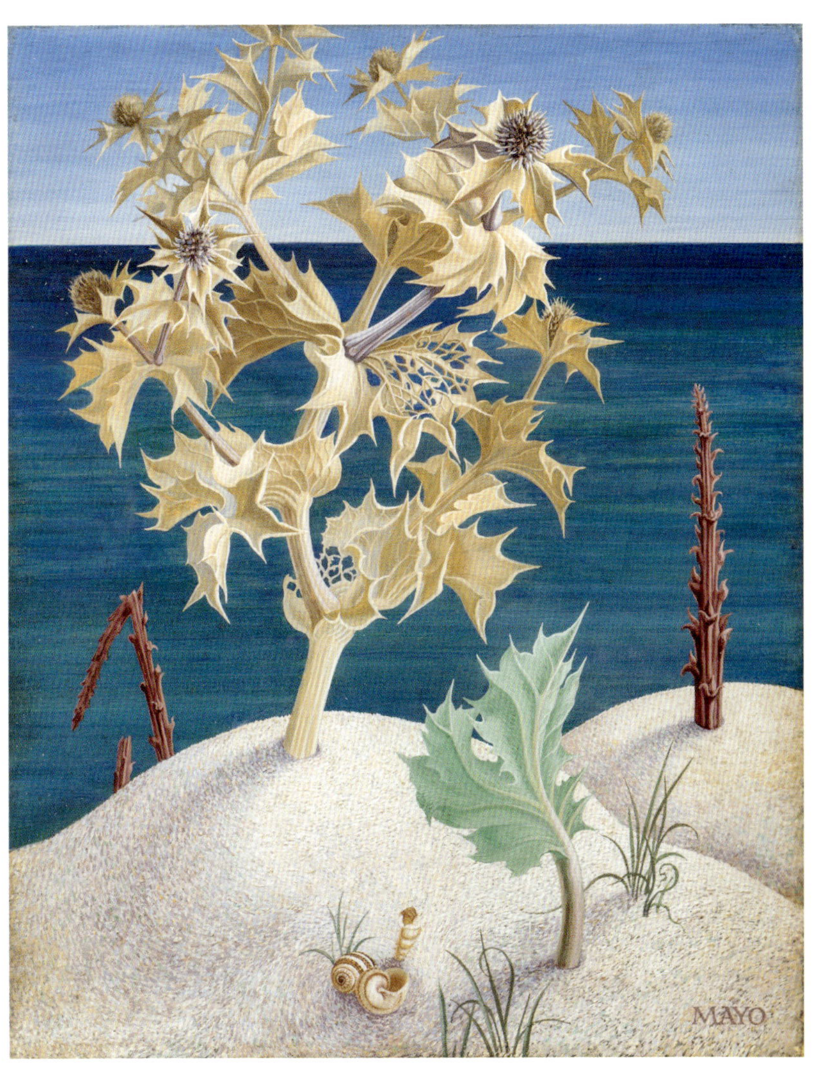

**17.** *Sea Holly No 1*, 1949, tempera on board

medium to master. There were few artists using tempera in the 1940s, largely because of rationing. For Mayo, its use for painting meant sacrificing the family's egg ration,[36] but it was perfect for her method of working, which required careful planning and precise execution. Her tempera works are some of her best paintings, for example, *Stage 17* (1948, Fig. 15), which was composed from a series of photographs taken by Mayo at Newhaven harbour, and again, has much in common with Ravilious's work made in the same location. Carrying through the theme of the fishing equipment, *Lobster Pot* (1950, Fig. 16) verges towards the surreal with its unusual perspective. One of her finest paintings, *Sea Holly No 1* (1949, Fig. 17), combines a sense of hyper-realism with elements of traditional surrealist painting. Depicting the spikey, sun-baked, sea holly central to the image, it is surrounded by snails and corals sitting on the sandy mound in front of the deep blue of the sea; the heat is almost palpable.

Despite the success of these works, Mayo never felt entirely at ease with painting, later conceding that it was not her strength. Her careful perfectionism and draughtsmanship overwhelmed the experimentation and freedom required for her to challenge her ambitions as a painter.[37]

## Tapestry Design

Mayo became interested in tapestry design following a visit to an exhibition of tapestries at the V&A in 1947.[38] The following year she travelled to France to study medieval tapestries, returning in 1949 to study at the Atelier Tabard in Aubusson, and also with the contemporary tapestry designer Jean Lurçat in Saint Céré.[39]

In 1949 Mayo attempted her own tapestry cartoon for a work entitled *Royal Avenue, Chelsea* (Fig. 18). This colourful, busy design combined personal interests – trees, leaves, animals and birds – but also figures and architecture. The scene, which

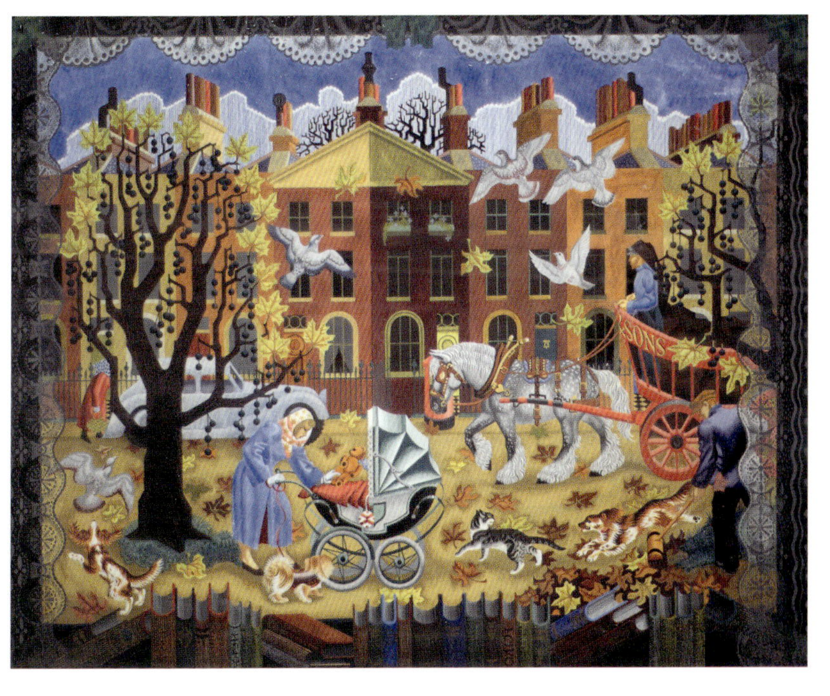

18. *Royal Avenue, Chelsea*, 1949, cartoon for tapestry; gouache on paper

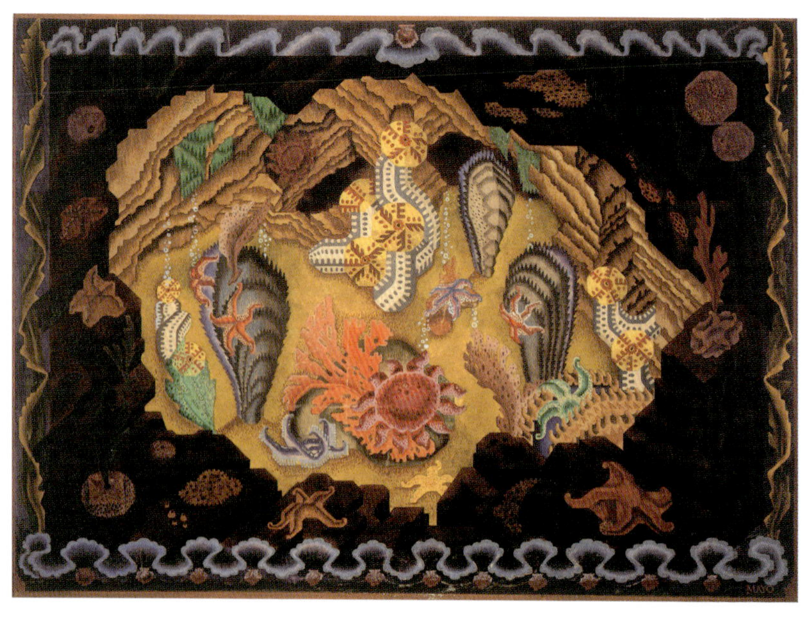

**19.** *Echinoderms*, 1950, woven tapestry

depicts the view through the window of Mayo's home studio, is framed by a bookshelf along the lower edge and lace curtains around the top and sides. The work exists only as a gouache on paper and was sadly never made into a tapestry.

After studying tapestry-weaving techniques at the Camberwell School of Art under Tadek Beutlich, Mayo went on to produce two further tapestry cartoons, *The Work of Women* (1950)[40] and *Echinoderms* (Fig. 19), the latter was the only realised tapestry design in her lifetime.[41] With its underwater design featuring starfish and sea-urchins, *Echinoderms* was woven in 1950 at the Dovecot Studios in Edinburgh, in preparation for its showing in the 1951 Festival of Britain English Tapestries exhibition at Birmingham City Art Gallery. It was one of several tapestries commissioned from designs submitted by artists including Graham Sutherland, Stanley Spencer, Duncan Grant and Vanessa Bell. This scheme was designed to support the Studios during the post-war financial slump and was also an attempt to revive interest in the medium.[42] It received support from the Arts Council, who from 1950 staged annual exhibitions of tapestries, and it is possible that Mayo's *Echinoderms*[43] hung in their London offices for a time following its inclusion in the exhibition tour.[44]

By this time Mayo had begun teaching drawing at St Martin's School of Art, and lithography and illustration at Sir John Cass College. She was also regularly exhibiting with the Society of Women Artists at the Royal Institute Gallery, at the Royal Academy and with the Royal British Artists, and her books were proving successful as well. She was spending an increasing amount of time in London and on her own work, and she could have continued with a steady career as an artist with a growing reputation in Britain. However, in 1952 following the breakdown of her marriage, Mayo took the decision to leave and move closer to her sister Josephine, who had settled in Sydney, Australia.

# Australia

Although she arrived in Sydney unhappy and feeling guilty for leaving her marriage, Mayo had planned ahead. In a letter to Ronald Cruickshank, Director of the Dovecot Tapestry Studios, written from aboard the ship bound for Australia, she noted: 'as far as work goes I have my hands full already. I signed a contract just before I left to write 10,000 words and do over 100 illustrations on a book on Marine Biology – A suitable subject to begin on an ocean voyage, which is what I am doing'.[45] She travelled on board the *SS Ixion*, a Blue Funnel cargo ship that took only 20 passengers and held no organised activities – perfect for Mayo as it enabled her to spend time focusing on her work. As she explained in the same letter, perhaps revealing some of her resentments regarding married life: 'It's a wonderful life, for a time at any rate. No shopping, cooking, washing or cleaning, yet somehow I am busy all day long.'[46]

The wildlife and natural history of Australia enchanted and inspired Mayo and it would prove to be a productive ten years during which she made a significant contribution to art and design. Her main source of income came from teaching illustration and drawing at the National Art School of Sydney, and she built up a network of friends and colleagues, particularly printmakers, including Hal Missingham, Director of the Art Gallery of New South Wales between 1945 and 1971.[47]

Her international reputation afforded Mayo respect and recognition among the art establishment in Australia, British art being popular and widely acquired there for public collections during the first half of the twentieth century. This, together with a revival of interest in printmaking, meant that Mayo was given plenty of exhibiting opportunities and her prints were received with great acclaim, winning numerous prizes including the Ku-ring-gai prize in 1960 for her 1953 work *Woman and Siamese Cat* (Fig. 20) – a rare self-portrait.

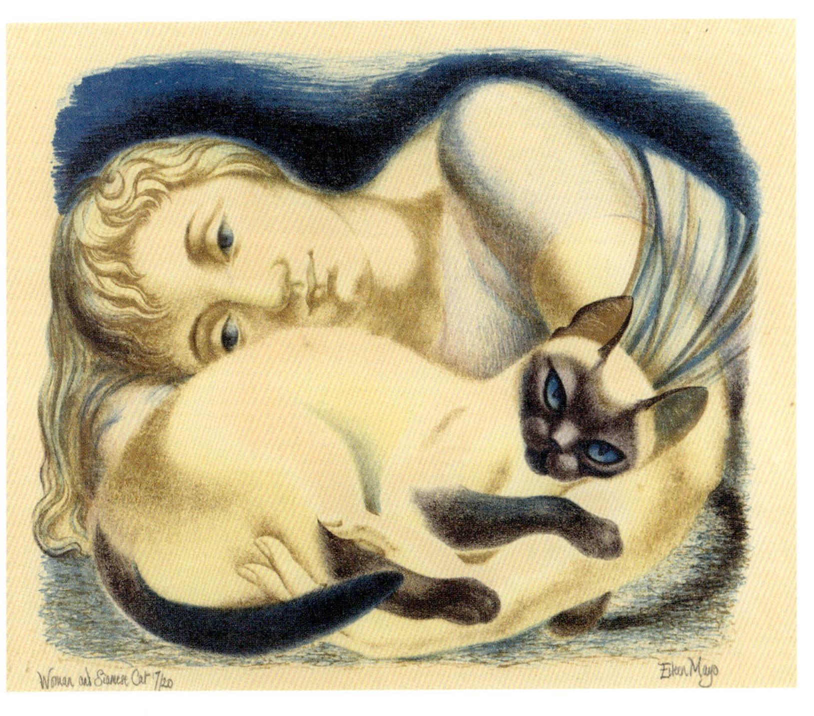


**20.** *Woman and Siamese Cat*, 1953, lithograph

Mayo was offered a wide variety of commercial commissions during this period, and out of financial necessity she accepted several, but as recognised by Cassidy, this did not please her.[48] It was arguably detrimental to her own creativity; her work at this time appeared to lack focus and consistent development as a result. However, the commissions were successful and always well-received.

One such project came from the Australian National Travel Association which invited Mayo to produce designs for travel posters advertising Australia as a tourist destination following the Second World War. She designed six colour posters using the offset lithography process, all of which featured a bold graphic typeface running along the bottom of the image, accompanied by illustrations of native animals and flora, including koalas, a kangaroo, a cockatoo and Sturt's Desert Pea. A slightly later poster was specifically designed for the Great Barrier Reef, Queensland, and included a vivid red coral, butterfly fish and a sea snail (Fig. 21). As with her South African works of the 1930s, Mayo went to great lengths to study the natural world of her immediate surroundings in order to gain a familiarity and understanding that she could bring to her prints and illustrations.

Throughout the late 1950s Mayo continued to design book-plates and posters, before becoming involved in designing murals and taking up stamp-design. She designed and paint-ed two murals: the first in 1959 for the Australian Museum in Sydney, for which she produced 55 paintings for a 9-metre-long installation called *The Tree of Invertebrates* (Fig. 22) to celebrate the centenary of Darwin's *The Origin of Species*; the second, in 1961, when she was invited to produce a mural for the main foyer of a new building being constructed for the Commonwealth Scientific and Industrial Research Organisa-tion (CSIRO) in Sydney. The accompanying booklet described how the mural 'was designed to depict the activities of the Division [of Food Preservation]. Diagrammatic representations

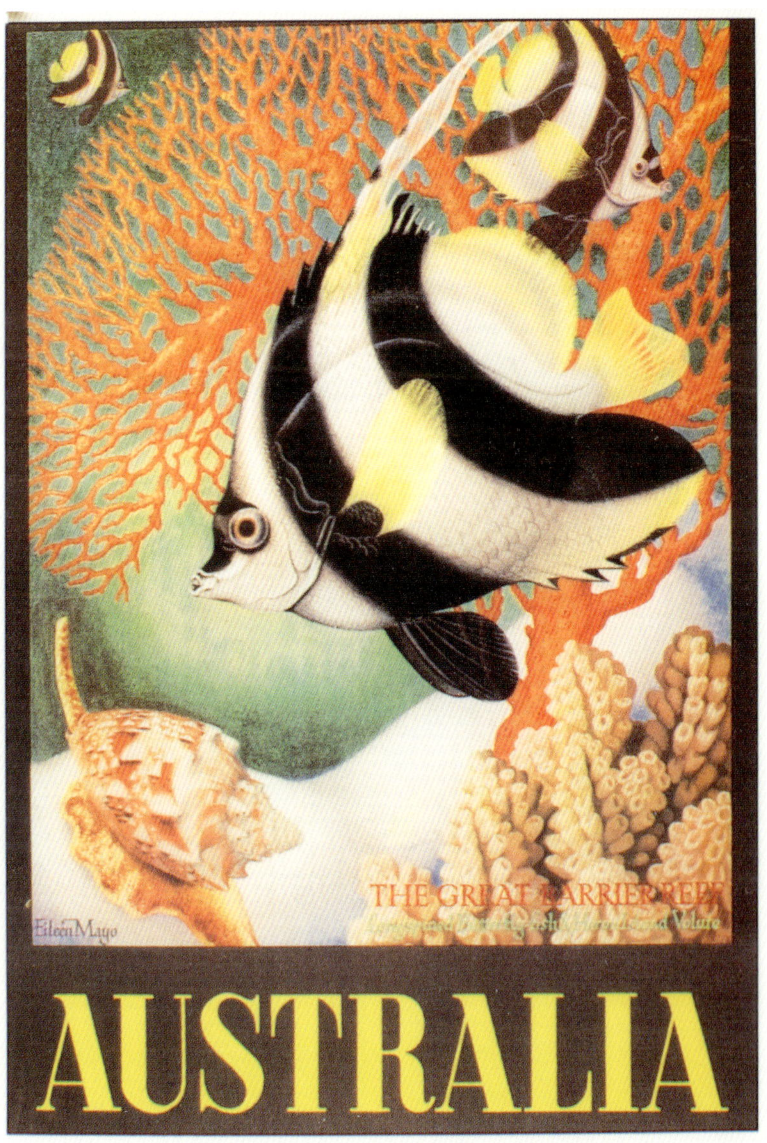


21. *Great Barrier Reef*, 1957, poster, offset lithography

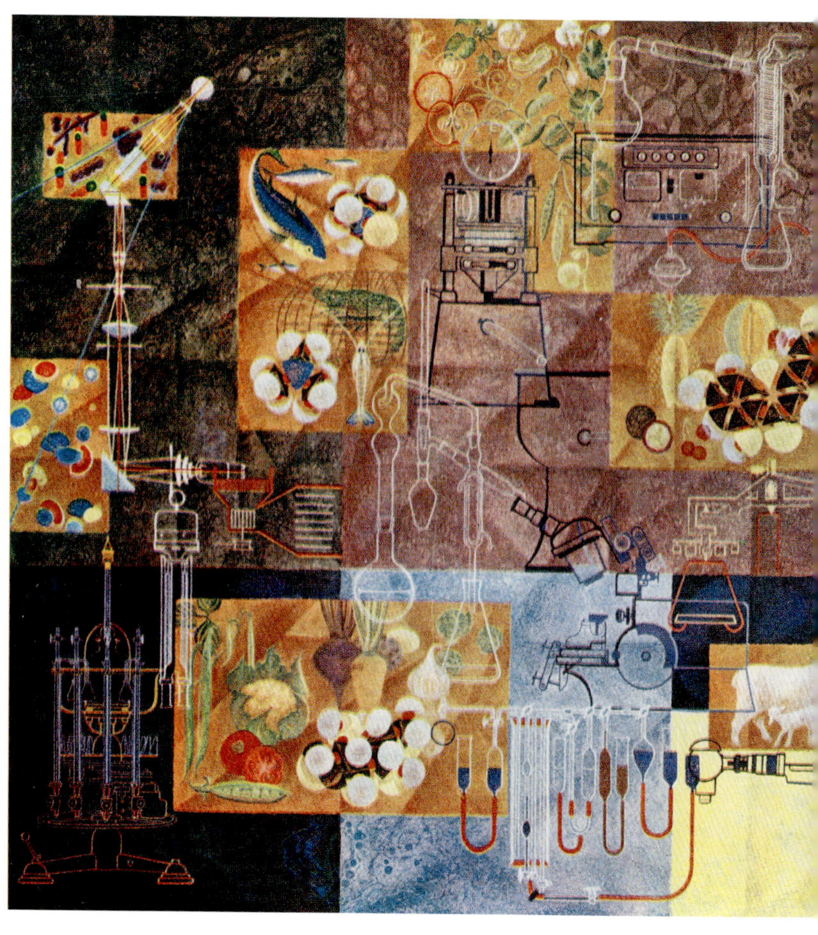

**22.** *The Tree of Invertebrates*, 1959, mixed media mural

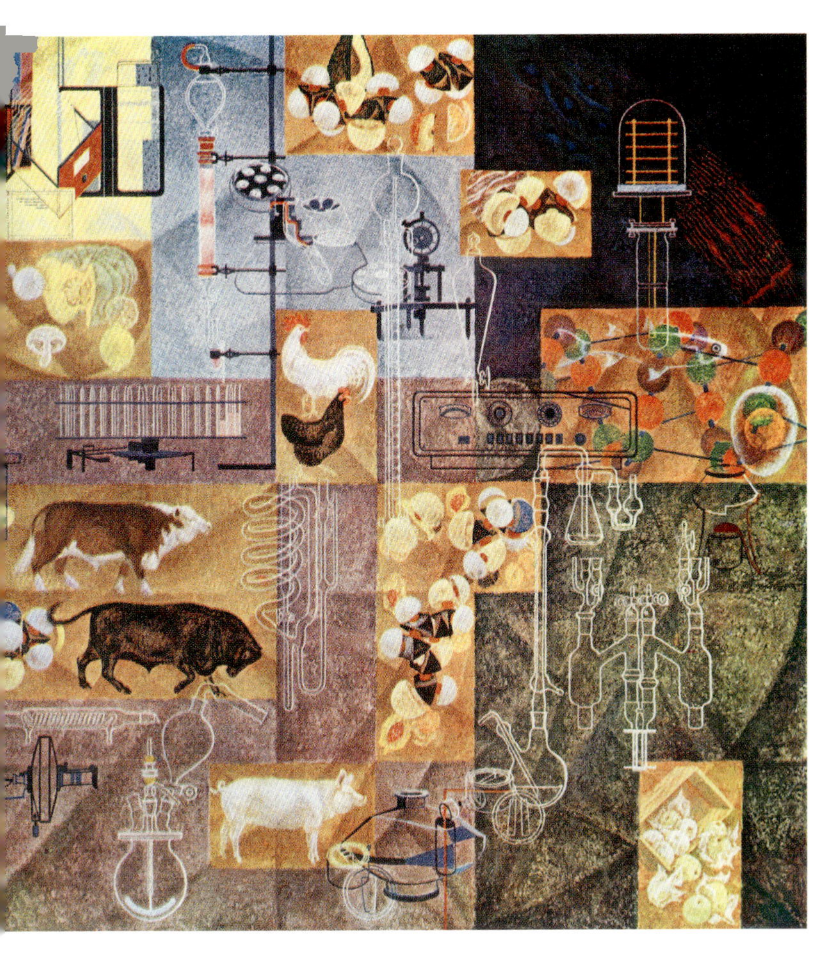

of laboratory apparatus overlie rectangles showing research materials and primary products: books, chemicals, micro-organisms, fruits, vegetables, animals, fish, poultry and eggs. Chemical compounds are represented by atomic models.'[49]

Another significant project begun by Mayo whilst still in Australia was her postage stamp commission. In 1957 she was invited by the Australian Stamp Advisory Committee to produce six designs that could be engraved for recess printing and reproduced in single colour. She submitted images of Australian mammals, including the kangaroo, koala, bandicoot and platypus, and was adamant that the designs must be 'striking, simple and up to date, without being gimmicky'.[50] The final stamps were deemed a great success and won her international recognition. She continued to design stamps in both Australia and in New Zealand over the next 30 years.


## New Zealand

Mayo made another significant move, this time to Waimate on New Zealand's South Island. By 1962, her mother, now in her eighties, needed increasing care, and Mayo's sister Margery had recently been widowed. Not for the first time, Mayo uprooted herself and started a new life, leaving behind a burgeoning artistic network. With similar enthusiasm to when she had moved from London to Sussex, the move from Sydney to the country town of Waimate seemed an opportunity to embrace rural landscape and wildlife once again. However, she soon realised that without access to the galleries and museums and an artistic community, her work would falter, and she eventually moved with her sister to the nearby city of Christchurch. Apart from a brief period living in Dunedin between 1972 and 1975, Mayo remained in Christchurch until her death.

The Australian stamp commissions lead to regular invitations from the New Zealand Post Office to produce first day covers, as well as stamps, for the Captain Cook bicentenary in 1969, and then for UNICEF and for the Antarctic Treaty anniversary. Having taken on work as a designer for Australia's decimal coinage, she also continued this work, designing coins for the New Zealand treasury.

While in Australia she had been one of the founding members of the Sydney Printmakers, and following her move, she continued printmaking with fervour, in time establishing herself in New Zealand. She also maintained an international presence, exhibiting in Switzerland in 1968 and Japan in 1969. It is during this period that her prints veer as far towards abstraction as she ever found herself; works such as *Winter Sleep* (1964, Fig. 23), *Summer Evening* (1967, Fig. 24), *Travellers* (1968), *Gently Floating Forms* (1970) and *Lunaria* (1972), show her freed somewhat from the realism of her former direct representation of nature and natural forms.

In order to devote herself to extending her print practice, Mayo designed herself a house and studio in 1975, which allowed her to widen her use of materials and techniques and experiment with different methods of relief printing. The giant sunflowers she grew in her garden provided inspiration for the acrylic paintings *Life Dance of Sunflowers* (1976) and *Sunflower Dance* (1979), as well as the print *Young Sunflower* (1979), for which she spent considerable time and effort perfecting the colours.

One of Mayo's final commissions involved producing thirty-six paintings of *Rare and Endangered Birds of New Zealand* (1976) for a series of cards for the Dunedin-based jelly manufacturer, Greggs. These collectable cards were inserted into an album divided up by habitat and would have given children an insight into the range of native New Zealand birds, as well as disseminating her work widely among a new and younger audience.

Mayo's passion for nature certainly made her a conservationist, but she was not by character an activist. However, the

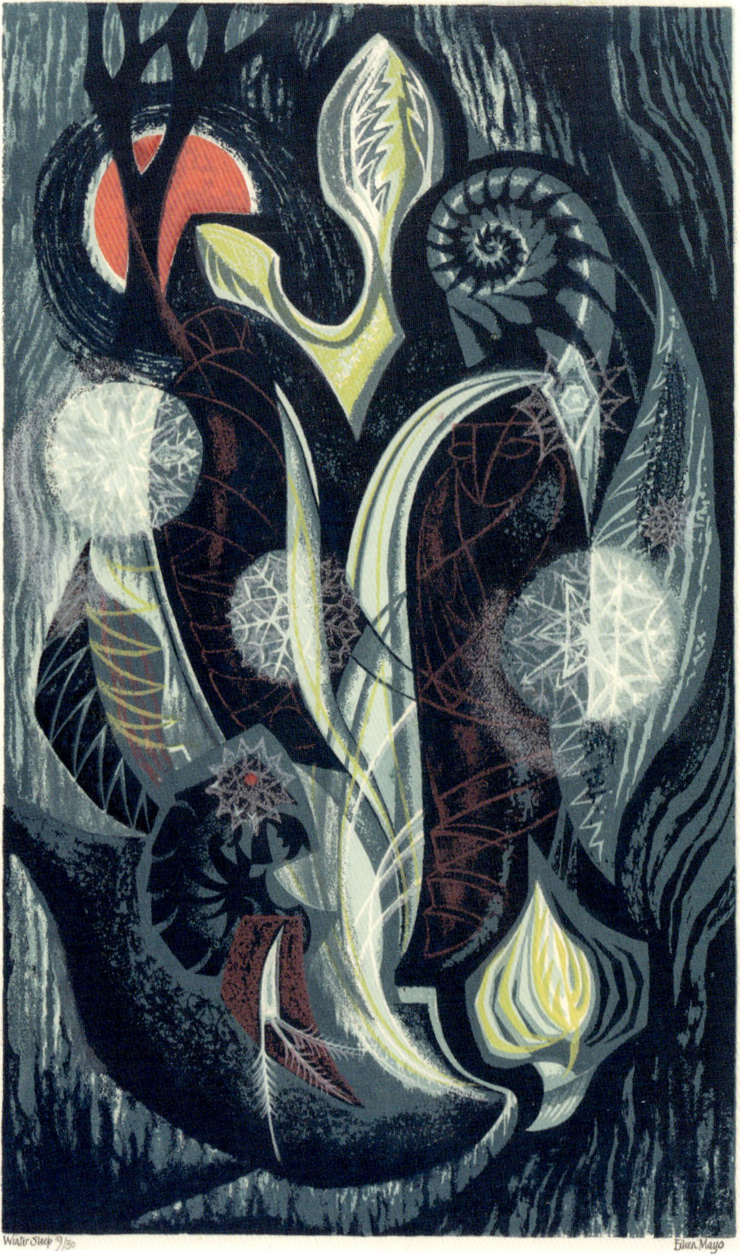

Winter Sleep 9/30                                                                                        Eileen Mayo

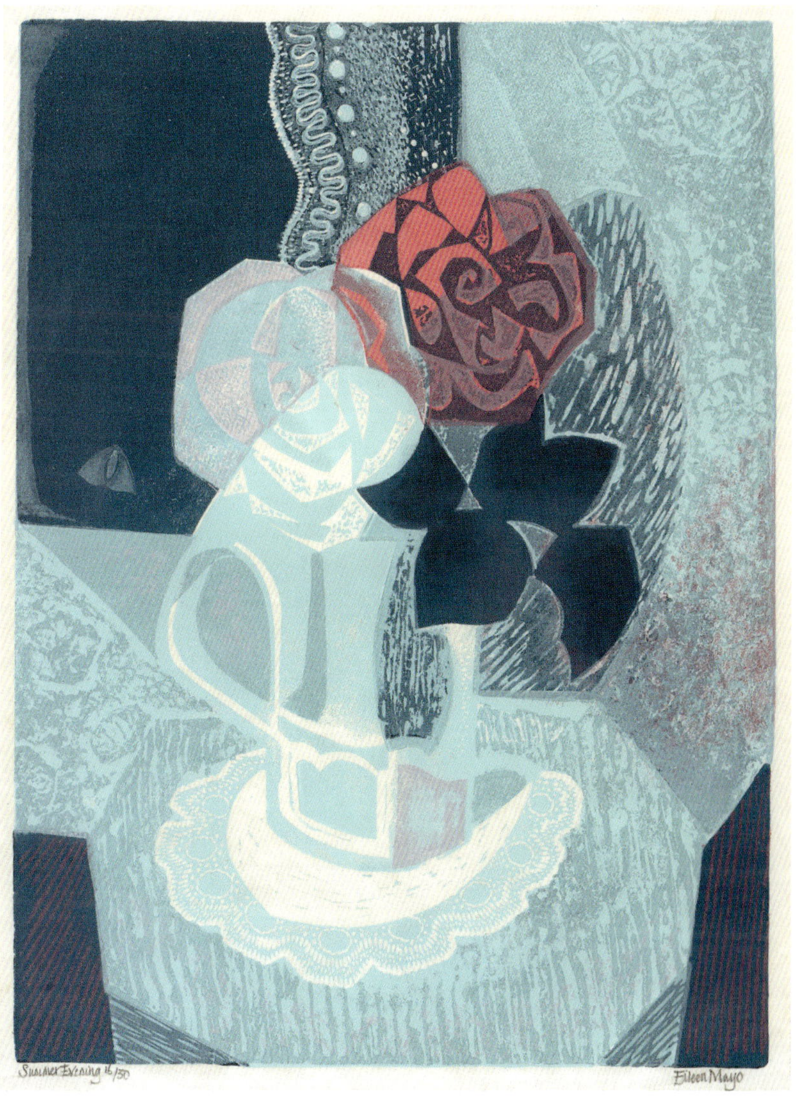


23. (opposite) *Winter Sleep*, 1964, screen print
24. (above) *Summer Evening*, 1967, lino-cut

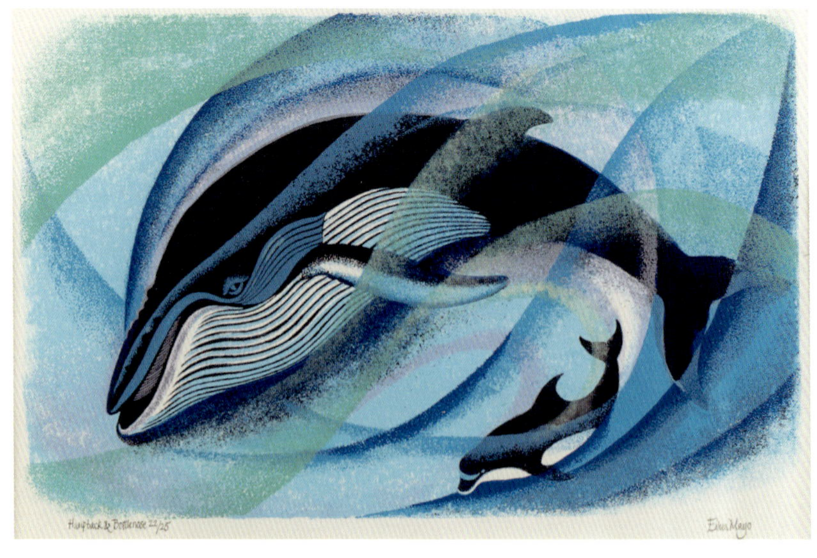

**25.** *Humpback and Bottlenose*, 1980, screen print

stranding of a large number of sperm whales on a beach near Auckland in 1974 had a significant impact on her and, combined with the continuation of Japanese whale hunting in the late 1970s and early 1980s, inspired her to produce the screen print *Humpback and Bottlenose* (1980, Fig. 25). She donated all the money from the sales of this print to the Save the Whales campaign,[51] and sent several editions of it to the New Zealand-based environmental organisation, Project Jonah.[52]

As with *Humpback and Bottlenose*, all of Mayo's late works were screen prints, this being the medium she then found easiest to use. During this period, she produced several accomplished and experimental prints including the graphic *Alphabets* (1982, Fig. 26), which she made in two colour ways. *Victorian Jug* (1984, Fig. 27), was a 7-screen print that was carefully composed to include a selection of her favourite flowers, including passion flowers and cornflowers, all arranged in a curved and decorative jug, contrasted with a squared, plaid tablecloth. For this print she employed a stippling technique that gave the work a softer appearance.

*White Cat and Poppies* was Mayo's final print, made in 1985 at the age of 79 (Fig. 28). Utilising the same stippling technique as in *Victorian Jug*, this work also brought together a number of her favourite subjects and pictorial techniques; the handsome white cat central to the image sits above striking ornamental poppies, all framed by lace curtains, as seen in her earlier work *Royal Avenue, Chelsea* (see Fig. 18).

Eventually Mayo stopped printmaking altogether as it became increasingly difficult due to her limited mobility and worsening arthritis.


## Legacy

Eileen Mayo left a significant and important legacy in each of the three main countries she lived – Britain, Australia and New Zealand. Whether or not this was recognised contemporaneously

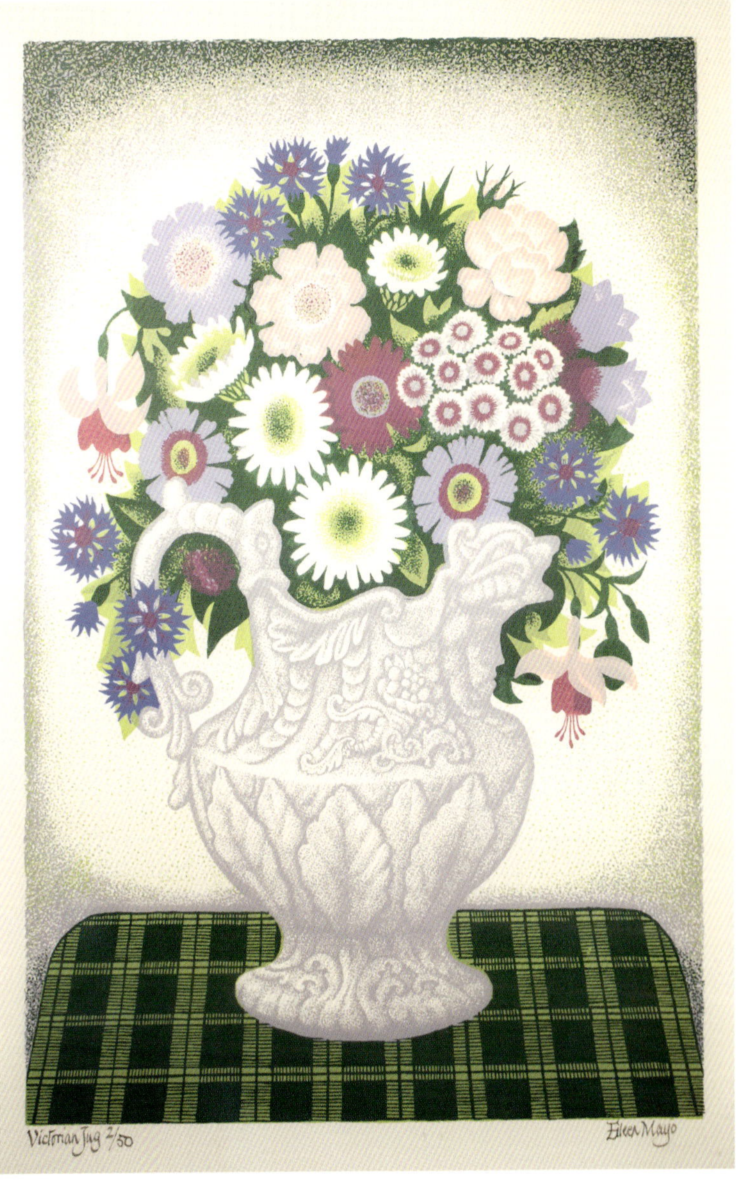



26. (opposite) *Alphabets*, 1982, screen print
27. (above) *Victorian Jug*, 1984, screen print

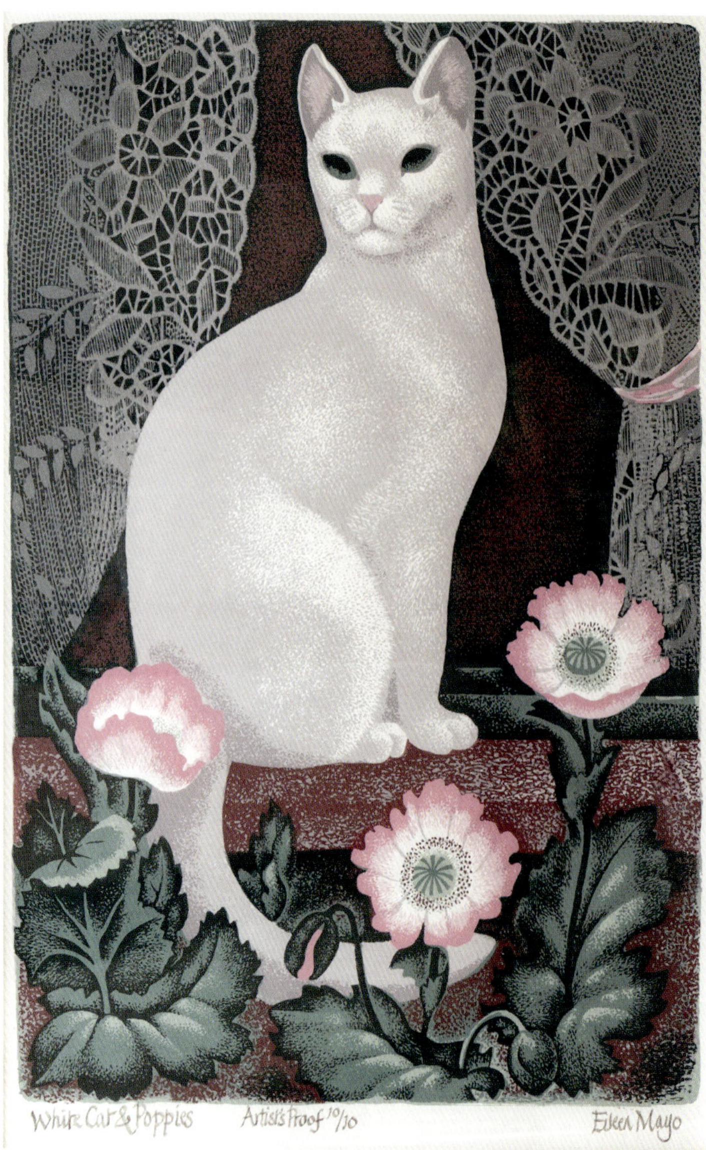


**28.** *White Cat and Poppies*, 1985, screen print

was largely due to the trends in art of the time and location, and not because her skill was ever in question. The Chancellor of the University of New South Wales, for which she produced the *Tree of Invertebrates* mural (see Fig. 22), described her as 'one of the world's leading natural history painters'.[53]

Mayo bucked many trends in her lifetime. Most notably, in an era when many Australian and New Zealand-born artists, including Frances Hodgkins, Sidney Nolan and Grace Cossington-Smith, moved to Britain, she conversely travelled in the opposite direction. It is testimony to her dedication and resilience that Mayo continued with her work after each move, forging new artistic networks and accepting ongoing commissions at every point.

She largely eschewed categorisation, maintaining her own approaches and ideas throughout her career. But like many British inter-war artists, such as Eric Ravilious, Tirzah Garwood, John Nash, Edward Bawden and Enid Marx, to name a few, Mayo worked across a wide range of medium. She mastered the traditional fine art skills – painting and drawing – as well as those usually thought of as design or craft, including wood-engraving, tapestry design, poster design and book illustration. Mayo saw no hierarchy in these disciplines and was equally skilled in all of them. She regarded painting as simply being a craft that needed to be mastered like any other, explaining in an article in 1949: 'We are so obsessed with the idea of painting being an ART that we forget, or even deliberately deny, that of its very nature (since it is not abstract but concrete) it is also a craft.'[54] For Mayo, that mastery developed through extensive research into technique, and also from gaining a thorough understanding of subject matter. Her rare ability to combine such in-depth knowledge of nature with considerable skill in representing this via a range of medium should have awarded her far greater recognition and appreciation.

This recognition eventually came in 1994, when Mayo was made a Dame of the British Empire in the New Year's Honours list – for services to the arts in New Zealand. Despite being over-looked and somewhat forgotten, particularly in Britain, this placed her alongside other women artists of note, including Dame Laura Knight, Dame Barbara Hepworth and Dame Eliza-beth Blackadder. The honour came just three days before she died on the 4 January 1994. According to Cassidy, who knew Mayo closely, it was questionable whether she would have accepted the DBE had it been offered to her earlier.[55] Aware of being somewhat overlooked in New Zealand, Mayo may have questioned the motivation behind the award. Highly self-critical throughout her long career, she would also have been wary of any unwanted publicity and attention encouraged by the award and the perception of her change in status.

While the DBE may have elicited mixed feelings, Mayo would undoubtably have been proud of the legacy that was created when her archives were preserved at the National Library of New Zealand and also at Tate Britain.[56] It is to be hoped that encouraging access to her work through these public archives, as well as through exhibitions of her work in the UK[57] and in New Zealand,[58] will bring a greater appreciation, and a wider recognition, of Mayo's oeuvre.

# Notes

1  Margaret Jillian Cassidy, *Shifting Boundaries: The Art of Eileen Mayo* (University of Canterbury PhD thesis, New Zealand 2000), p.23

2  Eileen Mayo, *Nature Diary*, 1920. Tate Archive, TGA 916-43

3  Ibid., 21 Feb 1920

4  This is perhaps not surprising given that Miss Rentoul was herself a graduate of the Slade School of Fine Art and Barton was active in pursuing his wider interests in art, architecture and design. Barton was, during the 1930s, an active member of the Design and Industries Association in Bristol, and a keen promoter of Modernism. He was an influential theorist and author of books including *Purpose and Admiration: A Lay Study of the Visual Arts* (London 1932) and *The Changing World: A Broadcast Symposium*, which was broadcast on BBC Radio in 1932.

5  *Sunday Dispatch* (24 April 1932), Tate Archive, TGA 916

6  See for example, *The Brass Goddess* (1929) and *Bric-a-Brac* (c.1929) by Harold Knight, and *Blue and Gold* (1927) by Laura Knight (Fig. 2).

7  *Daily Herald* (16 Sep 1930), Tate Archive, TGA 916

8  Alice Strickland, *Laura Knight* (Modern Women Artists, Eiderdown Books 2019)

9  Published in 1928–29, a number of these prints are now in the permanent collection of the V&A, given as part of the Cyril W. Beaumont Bequest.

10  Cassidy (cited note 1), p.227. The commission was for Beaumont's publication *The First Score: An Account of the Foundation and Development of the Beaumont Press* (London 1927).

11  Cassidy (cited note 1), p.39. *Review* (Feb 1930)

12  Edmund Blunden, *A Japanese Garland* (London 1930)

13  Cyril Beaumont, *Toys* (London 1930)

14  Cassidy (cited note 1), *Liverpool Post & Mercury* (3 Dec 1930), p.47

15  Cassidy (cited note 1), Letter to Stephen Coppell (3 Sep 1985), p.231

16  The Redfern exhibition was organised by its director Rex Nan Kivell, the New Zealand-born art collector. Later in life, when bequeathing his large art collection to public collections in New Zealand, Kivell included some of Mayo's early prints in gifts to the Christchurch Art Gallery and the Museum of New Zealand (Te Papa), Wellington.

17  *Daily Herald* (16 Sep 1930), Tate Archive 916

18  Ibid.

19  In conversation with Mayo's stepson (Aug 2021)

20  Dr Richard Gainsborough was well-educated and interested in the arts. In 1949, having retired as a GP, he established the magazine *Arts News and Review* (with Mayo designing the inaugural issue) that would later become *ArtReview*, as it is known today. He was keen to support his wife's career, retaining his son's nanny rather than expecting Mayo to take on full-time childcare duties.

21  Having attended Bristol Grammar School, Cleverdon would almost certainly have known Mayo's early mentor J.E. Barton and perhaps have been familiar with Mayo's early work. He had also curated a print exhibition for the Clifton Arts Club in Bristol in which Mayo had shown five prints.

22  JH Driberg (ed.), *The Bamboo Dancer and Other African Tales* (London 1937)

23  Medley's partner was the dancer Rupert Doone and together they founded the Group Theatre for which he would design the productions and sets, and for whom Moore designed a series of masks. This relationship to the theatre and dance would have appealed to Mayo given her earlier enjoyment of producing the Diaghilev ballet works for Cyril Beaumont. A portrait of Doone is reproduced in Alicia Foster, *Nina Hamnett* (Modern Women Artists, Eiderdown Books 2021).

24  Eileen Mayo, *The Story of Living Things and their Evolution* (London 1944)

25  Mayo (cited note 24), Prof Julian Huxley, Foreword, p.viv

26  Eileen Mayo, *Shells and how they live* (London 1944)

27  Eileen Mayo, *Little Animals of the Countryside* (London 1945)

28  Eileen Mayo, *Larger Animals of the Countryside* (London 1945)

29  Sally Carrighar, *One Day on Beetle Rock* (London 1946)

30  www.royalacademy.org.uk/art-artists/exhibition-catalogue/ra-sec-vol177-1945 (last accessed Aug 2021)

31  https://www.royalacademy.org.uk/art-artists/exhibition-catalogue/ra-sec-vol180-1948 (last accessed Aug 2021). A copy is also now in the V&A collection.

32  In conversation with Mayo's stepson (Aug 2021)

33  Cassidy (cited note 1), p.267

34  *Daily Mail* (13 Mar 1940), Tate Archive, TGA 916

35  Cassidy (cited note 1), p.114

36  Recalled in conversation with Mayo's stepson (Aug 2021)

37  Mayo's relationship with painting is discussed in further detail by Cassidy (cited note 1), p.138

38  *Masterpieces of French Tapestry* exhibition at the V&A, 29 Mar – 31 May 1947. Discussed in the ACE annual report 1946–47, p.19. See www.artscouncil.org.uk/arts-council-great-britain-2nd-annual-report-1946-7 (last accessed Aug 2021)

39  During this period in Paris, Mayo also studied life drawing with Ferdinand Léger at the Académie Montmartre.

40  Eileen Mayo, *The Work of Women* (1950). Gouache cartoon for unrealised tapestry.

41  According to a report in the *Falkirk Herald* (14 Mar 1953), *Echinoderms* measured 4ft4" by 5ft11" and was woven on 12 warps per inch. It took two weavers five months to complete and was finished in May 1951.

42  Discussed in conversation with Mayo's stepson (Aug 2021)

43  The *Echinoderms* tapestry is now in a private collection.

44  The recent discovery of a previously unknown Eileen Mayo tapestry cartoon, *Duck Pond*, has enabled the West Dean studios in West Sussex to commission and produce a full-size tapestry from the design. Similar to *Echinoderms* in its aerial perspective over the water, *Duck Pond*, with its vibrant mix of colours, depicts three ducks on the water, surrounded by dragonflies, frogs and newts, and the flora and fauna of a thriving pond. Mayo cleverly captured the difference in colours as the duck dives under the water.

45  Letter in Tate Archive, TGA 916

46  Ibid.

47  As well as having the same birth and death dates, there are a number of overlaps in the biographies of Mayo and Missingham: they both studied at the Central School of Arts and Crafts, with Noel Rooke and Bernard Meninsky, and both taught at Chelsea Polytechnic; although not documented, it is likely they knew each other before Mayo's move to Sydney.

48  Cassidy (cited note 1), p.84

49  Copy of the CSIRO booklet, Tate Archive, TGA 916-173. With the building yet to be finished, Mayo was brought in early to the planning discussions thereby enabling a complete cohesion between the architecture of the completed foyer and Mayo's mural design. Unfortunately, because she was unable to paint directly onto the walls (her preference for mural painting), she had to make the mural in own garage, using synthetic resin applied to panels of marine plywood, which were installed retrospectively.

50  Cassidy (cited note 1), p.182

51  Ibid., p.260

52  Project Jonah is a New Zealand-based environmental organisation set up in 1974, specialising in the protection and conservation of marine mammals.

53  *Melbourne Age* (24 Jul 1959). See Cassidy (cited note 1), p.212

54  Eileen Mayo, review of M. Maroger, *The Secret Formulas and Techniques of the Masters*, in *Art News & Review* (1947), Vol. I, no. 6, p.7

55  Cassidy (cited note 1), p.215

56  Tate Archive, TGA 916, was given by Mayo's stepson John Gainsborough, in 1991, and was accepted by the then Director, Nicholas Serota.

57  *Eileen Mayo* exhibition at Towner Eastbourne, 12 Feb – 3 Jul 2022

58  Most recently, *Eileen Mayo: Nature, Art and Poetry*, at Christchurch Art Gallery, New Zealand, 2 Feb – 16 Jun 2019.

# Image credits



1. Studio portrait photograph of Eileen Mayo by Marion Hoppé, *c.*1920–40, black and white print, 24.5 × 19.5 cm, Tate Archive, TGA 916/127 © Curatorial Assistance, Inc. / E.O. Hoppé Estate Collection. Photo: Tate
2. Laura Knight (1877–1970), *Blue and Gold*, 1927, oil on canvas, 51 × 46 cm, on loan to Penlee House Gallery & Museum © The Estate of Dame Laura Knight / Bridgeman Images.
3. Serge Lifar in George Balanchine's ballet Apollo Musagetes, Diaghilev Ballets Russes, 1928, drawing on paper, 38.6 × 21.9 cm, V&A, © Estate of Eileen Mayo/ Victoria and Albert Museum, London.
4. *Turkish Bath*, 1930, 4-colour lino-cut, 35 × 23 cm, private collection (photograph James Ratchford).
5. *Woman at a Dressing Table*, 1931, 5-colour lino-cut, 31.5 × 21.6 cm, private collection (photograph James Ratchford).
6. *Doric Dairy*, 1935, 5-colour lino-cut, 20.9 × 27.8 cm, private collection (photograph James Ratchford).
7. *Zulu Mother and Child*, 1935, conte crayon on card, 41.2 × 36.5 cm, private collection (photograph James Ratchford).
8. *Water Carrier*, 1937, 4-colour lino-cut, 31 × 22 cm, private collection (photograph James Ratchford).
9. *The Story of Living Things and their Evolution*, 1944, Waverley Book Company, London, private collection.
10. *Shells and how they live*, 1944, Pleiades Books, London, private collection (photograph Towner Eastbourne).
11. *Squirrel*, 1945, lithograph, 19.2 × 15.4 cm, private collection (photograph James Ratchford).
12. *Mending the Net*, 1949, Lithograph, 40 × 51 cm, private collection (photograph James Ratchford).
13. *Fletching Mill*, 1941, oil on canvas, 49 × 59.5 cm, private collection (photograph James Ratchford).
14. *Blue Nets*, 1950, oil on canvas, 61 × 44 cm, private collection (photograph James Ratchford).

15. *Stage 17*, 1948, tempera on oak panel, 50.5 × 40 cm, private collection (photograph James Ratchford).
16. *Lobster Pot*, 1950, tempera on oak panel, 41 × 32.5 cm, private collection (photograph courtesy of Deutscher and Hackett).
17. *Sea Holly No 1*, 1949, tempera on board, 41 × 33 cm, Auckland Art Gallery Toi o Tāmaki, The Ilene and Laurence Dakin Bequest, purchased 2014.
18. *Royal Avenue, Chelsea*, 1949, cartoon for tapestry; gouache on paper, 60 × 75.3 cm, Collection of the Aigantighe Art Gallery Gallery, New Zealand.
19. *Echinoderms*, 1950, woven tapestry, 183 × 137 cm, private collection.
20. *Woman and Siamese Cat*, 1953, lithograph, 83 × 34.3 cm, private collection (photograph John Hammond).
21. *Great Barrier Reef*, 1957, poster, offset lithography, 100.6 × 63.4 cm, private collection.
22. *The Tree of Invertebrates,* 1959, mixed media mural, 366 × 976 cm, Australian Museum, Sydney. Publication, Tate Archive TGA 916/173 © The estate of Dame Eileen Mayo, Photo: Tate.
23. *Winter Sleep*, 1964, screen print, 61 × 38 cm, Collection of Christchurch Art Gallery Te Puna o Waiwhetū, purchased 2005.
24. *Summer Evening*, 1967, lino-cut, 51 × 38 cm, Collection of Christchurch Art Gallery Te Puna o Waiwhetū, Gift of Prof. H. John Simpson and family, in memory of Ming Simpson, 2017.
25. *Humpback and Bottlenose*, 1980, screen print, edition of 25, 29.2 × 47 cm, private collection (photograph John Hammond).
26. *Alphabets*, 1982, screen print, edition of 35, 42.2 × 28 cm, private collection (photograph James Ratchford).
27. *Victorian Jug*, 1984, screen print, edition of 50, 56.1 × 36.6 cm, private collection (photograph James Ratchford).
28. *White Cat and Poppies*, 1985, screen print, 41.5 × 27 cm, private collection (photograph James Ratchford).

# About the author

Sara Cooper is Head of Collections and Exhibitions at Towner Eastbourne, where she is responsible for the exhibition programme and for the permanent collection, including overseeing acquisitions. She has curated numerous exhibitions, including *John Nash: The Landscape of Love and Solace* (2021) and its forerunner, *Ravilious & Co: The Pattern of Friendship* (2017) (both created in collaboration with Andy Friend), as well as *David Nash: 200 Seasons* (2019), *Phoebe Unwin: Iris* (2019), *Peggy Angus: Designer, Teacher, Painter* (2014) and *Harold Mockford: A Retrospective of a Sussex Painter* (2012), for which she also produced and wrote the accompanying exhibition catalogue. Previously she was Curator at the Sainsbury Centre for Visual Arts, Norwich. She has two MAs from the University of East Anglia in Museology and in Modern European Art, and a BA (hons) in Linguistics and Art History.

# Acknowledgements

It has been a privilege to work on this publication about Eileen Mayo, about whom little has been written in this country. The insights from John Gainsborough and family, have been invaluable, and our meetings thoroughly enjoyable. Mayo's great niece Dr Lucie Stanford, based in Australia, has also been a great help. Thanks also go to Mayo's New Zealand-based friend and biographer Jillian Cassidy, for her support and generosity. The initial suggestion for a Mayo exhibition at Towner Eastbourne came from Caroline Collier, who saw the potential for a meaningful fit of artist and institution, for which I'm extremely grateful.

A number of museums and galleries have been helpful with their supply of images and information, including Katie Herbert, Curator and Deputy Director at Penlee Art Gallery, and Geoffrey Heath and Sophie Matthiesson at Auckland Art Gallery.

My personal thanks go to my friends and colleagues at Towner Eastbourne, and to Karen Taylor for our conversations about why this book was important. I am grateful to Harriet Olsen, founder of Eiderdown Books, for enabling me to be part of this special series alongside several women writers and curators whose work I admire. Thanks go to my family, to all the brilliant women who I am fortunate to count as friends, to Glen for his love and endless support, and to the two best modern women in my life – Charlotte and Annabelle.

# Index

Eileen Mayo
By Sara Cooper
First Edition

First published in the United Kingdom in 2021 by Eiderdown Books
Eiderdownbooks.com

Series conceived and developed by Eiderdown Books
Text © Sara Cooper
Images © The estate of Dame Eileen Mayo. All rights reserved.
Additional © see Image credits

The moral right of the author has been asserted.



Every effort has been made to ensure images are correctly attributed however if any omission or error has been made please notify the publisher for correction in future editions.

A CIP record for this book is available from the British Library.

ISBN: 978-1-9160416-8-4

Edited by Rebeka Cohen
Indexed by Jan Worrall
Series design by Clare Skeats
Typeset by Nicky Barneby in Lelo by Katharina Köhler

The Modern Women Artists logotype is set in Hesse Antiqua which was released in 2018 to mark the 100th birthday of Gundrun Zapf von Hesse. The forms of Hesse Antiqua are based on the metal punches that von Hesse created in 1947 while working as a bookbinder at the Bauer Type Foundry in Frankfurt.

Printed and bound by Latitude
Reprographics by ALTA

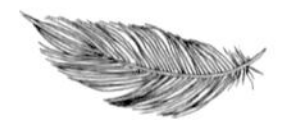